Off the Farm

ISBN 0-9657578-3-8

Photograph of saguaro cactus on page 73 by Glenda Bergeson. Photograph of the author as a first grader on page 171 by Paul Bergeson. Remaining photographs by the author.

Contents

CHAPTER ONE

OFF TO TOWN

Alone in a Crowd

One thing missing in small towns: public spaces where one can remain alone. To maintain privacy in a small town, you have to hide in your house and unplug your phone.

The city, for all of its annoyances, offers plenty of places to hide besides your home. Shopping malls, parks, city streets, book stores–you can hang out for days without running into somebody you know. People-watching opportunities abound.

I find it easier to read or write in a public place than at home. At home, one's accumulated possessions conspire to pull one away from work. When one works in a cafe, the hours blissfully and productively dissolve. The busy buzz of background noise has a narcotic effect.

Small towns usually have a cafe or two, but nobody would ever think of reading there. The last time anybody tried that around here was in July of 1976. A hairy guy from the carnival sat up at the counter and read a naughty-looking novel for about an hour. What a relief when he left so everybody could quit staring and finish their pie.

So, reading at the cafe wouldn't work, even though I am local and not very hairy. It would seem pretentious, something an idealistic English major home for the summer might try.

I enjoy bringing my laptop computer to coffee shops in the city. I can sit there and work for hours and nobody says boo. Try that in the small town and you're asking to be mumbled about. What's he trying to prove? Suppose we'd better be quiet so Mr. Important can work on his memoirs.

Any attempt to concentrate would be aggressively sabotaged. S'pose you've been pretty busy, then. Whatcha reading? Whatcha workin' on? Whatcha been up to? What kinda machine is that?

Big city cafes have their own problems, especially now that every Tom, Dick and Harry finds it necessary to carry a cell phone. People assume they have a right to talk loudly wherever and whenever those things ring. When they do, I stare angrily until they walk away. That usually works, but it isn't a trick I would try on the dice-shakers at the local cafe.

Pretty tough to people-watch in the small town, too. You can sit on a bench on Main Street and watch the cars go by on a Saturday night, but you've seen them all before and you end up waving to most of them and then you spend the next week answering questions about what you were doing sitting on that bench last Saturday.

This is as it should be. Small towns are cozy places. The people are basically warm-hearted. They might gossip about you, but when you die, they come to your funeral. En masse. Especially if there's good food.

Yet, sometimes I wish I wouldn't have to go so far to sip coffee and read a book where there's little chance of being noticed, or watch people whose stories I don't already know.

Small Town Funerals

However low the rural economy sinks, let's hope small towns never lose their ability to throw a good funeral.

Oddly, one of the great comforts of a small town is the way people turn out for funerals, even for the very elderly. In the city or the suburbs, I doubt that you could fill half-a-room for a funeral of a 90-year-old, but in the small town, a full house is common.

In the city or suburbs, older people disappear from community life, what there is of it, when they retire. In the small town, people usually remain a part of the social fabric as long as they don't move away.

So, when an older person passes away in the small town, a whole bunch of people feel as if they lost a friend. People of all ages, faiths, and social groups fill up the old country churches with crowds seldom seen on a Sunday morning.

Most older people have been a part of the scenery for the entire lives of those younger than they. They almost attain historic landmark status. They saw you grow up. You remember when they still lived on the farm. Lately, you have run into them at the store, at the cafe, or at other funerals.

Even though you might have only four or five brief chats with a person per year, those little exchanges build up over the decades. Hearing of an older person's death can bring back poignant memories even if you weren't all that close.

Most of those memories are good. Some are mixed with guilt. Poor Lars, I wonder if he ever found out I was in on the plot to fill his car with live pigeons. Or if Emil found out that it was me who called him late one night pretending to be an Amway salesman.

And I wonder if Martha ever found out that I put a earthworm in her soda thirty years ago. Martha, as it happens, later died of throat cancer. As an eight-year-old, I was haunted by the thought that it was the worm which caused her illness.

But if you stay around town long enough, you have time to grow up and repair relations with most everybody. You have to, or life can become a daily obstacle course of guilt and resentment.

Watching people near you go from positions of power and vitality into old age makes one realize that the same thing will someday happen to you. The dawning awareness that we all share the same fate tends to breed civility in once brash youth.

Funerals bring together the community to see the best in one of its members. Uncomfortable memories are tactfully avoided as the need to forgive and forget is brought home forcefully without a word being said to that effect.

Of course, the scrumptious food at small-town funerals isn't a minor matter. Not only is the food delicious, but it is unabashedly decadent. There might be six dishes called 'salads,' but not a shred of lettuce pollutes any one of them. Just jello, whipped cream and marshmallows, maybe a can of pineapple.

Coffee, cake, and loud chatter in the old church basement cap off the funeral ritual on a less than somber note. Everybody is on their best behavior, spiffed up, kind and considerate. The next-of-kin part, one hopes, with a sense that their loved one mattered to many.

With each old-timer's death, a little chunk of the way things were disappears. A set of stories is silenced. A bit of wisdom is lost.

But the funeral itself brings out the best small towns have to offer. Here's hoping that small town funerals–with their tater-tot hotdishes, jello salads and sturdy ceramic coffee cups–long endure.

Waving Skills

It is a singularly small town talent, and one I lack: the ability to recognize oncoming cars soon enough to decide whether or not to wave.

I would like to take this opportunity to apologize to all of you who have waved to me as we met at 120 miles-per-hour. I didn't mean to snub you. My intentions were good. In fact, I probably waved after we passed and then spent the next couple of minutes hoping your feelings weren't hurt.

But all cars look the same to me, particularly when whizzing my way. To recognize an oncoming vehicle soon enough to issue a convincing wave seems to me a skill on par with hitting a Nolan Ryan fastball. I am just not that good.

I could wave to everybody, I suppose, but that seems promiscuous. Instead, I have divided area highways into waving roads and non-waving roads.

Waving roads are side roads near home. On these roads, the odds are so high that I will know the person in the oncoming car that I just go ahead and wave at every one. I know that this means I might wave at a strange car every now and then, but that is a risk I'll have to take.

It goes without saying that all gravel roads are waving roads, even those so narrow and frostboiled that you would be wiser to keep both hands gripping the wheel as you meet. Not waving to a neighbor on a bad gravel road is a snub that could start a long-running feud. Wave on gravel, even if it means risking a head-on crash.

However, I consider major trunk highways and any highway more than twenty miles from home to be non-waving highways. If you meet me on a non-waving highway, don't expect much, and please don't think I am stuck up.

The talent for recognizing oncoming cars knows no gender distinction, and it is not genetic. Both my mother and sister have the talent of recognizing cars, but somehow I missed out.

Small towns are filled with experts on recognizing oncoming cars, so much so that I fully expect the Department of Homeland Security to tap small town people to help with the fight against car bombers and other forms of terror.

In fact, I feel like these people are spies already.

Who needs the FBI when you have locals who can say with confidence, "What were you doing down by Barnesville last Thursday? I met you on Highway 9." I feel like asking, do you have my phone bugged, too?

I am just lucky to find my vehicle in the West Acres parking lot without first sticking my key in the locks of several other pickups vaguely similar to my own. And those vehicles aren't moving.

Once, while visiting a relative in California, I borrowed a car to go to Barnes and Noble—and forgot what the car I borrowed looked like. I stuck my key in the locks of so many cars that I was sure security would pull me in for questioning.

I can tell a pickup from a car. That much I understand. But the difference between a Buick and a Mercury eludes me. And all of these monster SUVs look like tanks. Not a one of them stands out.

It is clear that I suffer from VRDD (Vehicle Recognition Deficit Disorder). As a victim of VRDD, I ask you to be understanding of my sometimes erratic behavior in highway waving situations. I am powerless over the situation, and am trying to find help.

Small Town Driving

Has anybody ever figured out the driving rules for small towns? Are there any? Are they ever enforced?

As far as I can tell, it is each person for themselves. If you live in one place long enough, you begin to learn everybody's rules. When you see Elmer's yellow Malibu coming down the road, you know just what to expect.

But if you are from out of town, look out. Drive into a small town at your own risk. Consider your life to be in peril.

Elmer doesn't cross intersections even if he has the right-of-way. He's retired. To Elmer, the young whippersnapper in the new pickup across the intersection looks like he's in a hurry. Probably has important business. So, it is Elmer's policy to just sit at the intersection until things settle down a bit, then he'll pull out.

Locals understand Elmer's driving behavior, but outsiders wait impatiently for him to take advantage of his right-of-way. They honk, gesture and yell–none of which does any good, since Elmer is hard of hearing and doesn't see real well, either.

Mavis creeps along in her 1973 Oldsmobile, but stops for nothing. She rolls through stop signs, onto the busy highway, back onto the back streets, all at an excruciatingly stately pace. When you see Mavis, get out of the way.

Mavis is a particular problem for semis which roar through town loaded with snowmobiles, grain or windows. She yields for nothing. You wonder if she knows how many times she has caused the abrupt hiss of air brakes, or inspired streams of profanity.

Oscar parks five feet from the curb, but Norbert parks with one or more wheels on the curb. Ophelia parks parallel in the diagonal, and Matilda uses the handicapped zone at the grocery store even though she doesn't have a sticker.

The use of turn signals in small towns is completely optional, mainly because most people don't decide until the last minute which way they are turning. That's what stop signs are for–to give you time to evaluate your turning options. Once you decide, it is too late to signal anyway.

One local legend used to work her way out of tight spots with her Impala by ramming the cars in front of her and behind her until she worked her way free. As far as anybody knows, nobody ever filed a claim against her. If you were stupid enough to park in front of Eleanora's green Impala, you deserved what you got.

Yes, it is dangerous to drive in a small town. It would be a lot safer if all of the drivers possessed all of their faculties.

But we all know each other's rules. We know what to expect. If outsiders can't handle a little variety in driving behavior, they should move away or take another route.

It is a sad day when I hear that another local driver has had their keys taken away. The local streets may be made safer, but the town loses a little flavor.

Church Dinners

Fall is the season for church dinners. Catholics, Method-ists, Presbyterians, all the various flavors of Lutherans, ev-erybody seems to have their dinners in October. I suppose that is when people are the most hungry. The weather is cooling off, and the body is telling us to put on that extra winter padding.

There could probably be greater inter-faith cooperation to avoid overlapping dinners, but I suppose that is asking a bit much. You can't have it all. You can't have your meatballs and expect ham, too.

I choose church dinners by food rather than doctrine. Meatball suppers always tempt me. Ham never fails. Turkey is fine, but barbecue of any sort will lure me for sure.

I regard lutefisk as a toxic substance. Let's hope terrorists never get ahold of it, they could paralyze the entire country. I take long detours around lutefisk suppers, just to be safe.

No church wants to be seen as stingy. They load up the plates till they overflow, particularly if you are a male under forty years of age.

Come back for seconds, they say, there's plenty more in back. There's more potatoes in the oven. We've got way too much cole slaw. Help yourself. Did you get pickles? Aren't you having cake? We have way more beans than we need, take more for crying out loud.

Dessert presents a problem. Here comes the plate loaded with ten scrumptious kinds of cake. German chocolate with brown sugar and coconut frosting, lemon-filled white cake, carrot cake with cream cheese frosting, angel food cake with speckled frosting, the works.

But how do you pick when there are six ladies watching you choose? Each one of them, I suspect, brought a cake. Nobody will say which one is theirs. If I choose one over the others, is somebody going to be hurt?

I used to feel bad for the woman who made the cake nobody takes, usually a white cake with an off-color frosting. What if she goes home with a pan full of cake—will the rejection push her over the edge? Shouldn't there be counselors available for that sort of thing?

Lately, I have decided that life is too short. You can't have your cake and eat it, too, they say, but you can make sure to eat the piece of cake you want when you have the chance.

I compliment all of the rejected cakes before giving my reason for taking the one I want. This piece is smaller, and I am already full. Chocolate makes me hyper. I had carrot cake for breakfast. Angel food makes my stomach hurt. Better not take the banana bar, Mervin has his eye on it.

But you know, the ladies probably don't care. For them, this is church dinner #425. Some cakes work, other cakes don't. If there's some left, they'll just take it home and let the old man work on it for the rest of the week.

County Fair

The county fair is the small-town equivalent of Mardis Gras, a time when it is permissible for respectable people to stay out late and indulge in exotic pleasures such as cheese curds, elephant ears and Rocky Road ice cream without doing permanent harm to their reputation.

The usual rules are suspended at the county fair. The same overprotective parents who might be expected to require a criminal background check for a baby-sitter suddenly are willing to hand their toddler over to a cigarette-puffing carnie so dirty and hairy that it is difficult to tell where the grease leaves off and the tattoos begin.

Non-gamblers throw darts to win a stuffed bear for the wife. Dieters stuff themselves with greasy burgers. Grandmas bedecked in polyester pantsuits hang out near rides which blare songs by AC/DC and the Village People.

Sellers of vitamin supplements, dubious cure-all potions, unproven fuel additives, leftover flowers, cheap jewelry and bad food all descend upon the county fair in search of a quick buck. Many frugal locals, their purse strings loosened by the spirit of the moment, buy things that they won't admit to later.

The crowning event of the fair, the demolition derby, turns small town values completely upside down. For one night per year it is permissible for the town's young people to bash into each other's cars, spin their wheels, shake their fists, rap their pipes, and raise up clouds of blue smoke.

Not only is the demolition derby legal, but the the same

solid citizens who normally call the cops at the first screech of a tire actually pay five dollars per head to watch.

Some nice kids enter the derby, but they usually get caught up on the sand pile before their car sees a dent. The prize inevitably goes to a greasy wrench twister from the wrong side of the tracks who couldn't spell the word valedictorian if he were paid. And the crowd roars.

There is virtue on display at the fair, too. The crafts barn oozes wholesomeness. It is comforting to know that some people still care enough about jelly-making to be angry that their jar got a red ribbon. The woodcarvers competition always draws oohs and ahs.

The 4-H barns remind us that some people out here still raise animals. The courteous, wholesome farm kids who carefully comb their horses provide a nice contrast to the foulmouthed junior high gangs on the midway.

The friendly folks at the Gospel Booth remind us that the end is near. The evidence is not only to be found in present-day Mideast politics, but right out here on the midway where hip-hop music is being pounded into our children's brains while parents stand by numbly complacent.

Sandwiched between the extremes of Good and Evil so prominently on display at the county fair are a whole bunch of Lutherans who just come to visit. They gather in and around the Ladies Aid food stand. Once they get a good spot, they don't move.

Unfazed by the temptations of the midway, unmoved by the prophets of doom, the solid citizens greet old friends and talk amongst themselves about the nice weather and how good the crops look.

By early Monday afternoon most out-of-town visitors have vamoosed. The carnival has packed up and left. The tents have all been folded. The litter has vanished. The pounding music has been silenced, and the town belongs to the solid citizens once again.

Class Reunion

A class reunion is an event many approach with equal parts anticipation and dread. Some just skip it, others come reluctantly. My twenty year reunion was held last weekend. I would never miss it, although attending stirred some old anxieties.

It is good to see everybody, but jumping back into the pool of people with whom you endured the horrors and humiliations of ages five through seventeen isn't for everyone. One might think: so much has changed. I am more content now than I was then. Why go back?

The organizers of class reunions are usually the same ones who did all the work for prom. They confront apathy, resistance and hostility at every turn.

If they have some dumb program, I am not going to come. Forget it, I am not going to write down my life history for everybody to read. No thanks, I do not care to be nominated for the hair loss award. Let's just have some food, visit a while and call it good.

Others decide that, stop to think of it, the ones I want to keep in touch with I already am in touch with.

For these reasons, it is tough for the organizers to get an accurate head count. Most people want to leave their options open until they get a feel for who else is going. Skittish spouses sign up and then back out. The rebels, if they come, just show up at the last minute.

But the indefatigable organizers soldier on, just as they

did in high school, planning for food, decorations, pictures, gag prizes, and a DJ to play favorites from the early 80s.

The event itself was fun. I was nominated for the hair loss award, but did not win. My consolation prize was a cheap set of curlers. My single status won me a plastic barbie doll bride.

There was a brief class trivia quiz, which flopped. Most people want to just forget the old nicknames. Not a soul remembered the prom theme, can you imagine that. Our class motto was some mushy clap-trap about hopes and dreams.

The DJ thought we were the class of 1972 and played stuff like "Smoke on the Water" until somebody set him straight. He more than made up for his mistake with AC/DC's "Dirty Deeds Done Dirt Cheap." The dance floor filled. Selections from the works of Cindy Lauper, Meatloaf, and the J. Giles Band followed.

In between, snippets of conversation with classmates. You still in Fargo? Yep. So how do you like it? Oh, its fine. Yep. Pretty good, actually. Yep. So, not a bad turnout! Nope. Not bad. Yep. Nope. Yep.

Well, I'd better go get another barbecue here. Yep, okay then. See you. Yep. Have a good one.

Superficial conversation, sure, but that's about all the deeper one wants to get or you end up in the touchy territory of divorces, chemical dependency, loss of jobs, politics, religion and so on. There is safety in small talk.

Yep. So the reunion went pretty good. Not bad at all. Kinda fun, actually. Good to see everybody. Yep. Good food. Probably have to go to the next one. If I'm around. Yep. Nope. Well, I suppose I better be going here.

Busy Kids

On a recent perfect April morning, with temperatures approaching seventy degrees, I happened to stop by an area school building. I was surprised to find the dank gymnasium swarming with dozens of grade school children, accompanied by their parents, coolers in tow.

It was a basketball tournament. On a Saturday. In April. For elementary students, some of whom had traveled for hours to get there.

What is going on here? Shouldn't a Saturday in April be a time when grade school children scurry outside to catch frogs, dam up creeks, and generally get into mischief? Shouldn't their parents be out in the yard raking leaves or washing windows? What perverse logic drives entire families to spend a perfect April Saturday in a smelly gym?

I am appalled by how organized childhood has become. Activity after activity. After-school programs for all ages. Organized, competitive sports for near tots. Not even Saturdays or evenings are sacred!

These days, the thought of allowing a child a free, unplanned moment seems to fill parents with fear and trembling. Programs, dance line, organizations, clubs, play dates, elaborate parties. You wonder when kids get time to just explore the neighborhood.

People want to do everything for their children, but they forget that the best thing they could do is have interests of their own and provide a close up example to their children of a person who has a life.

Modern children—those lucky enough to have a reasonably solid family—seem to be excessively monitored, controlled, regimented, doted upon, scheduled, kept track of, spoiled. Their parents seem to have nothing better to do.

The children look dazed to me. Perhaps kids instinctively realize that their success on the basketball court, even as a fourth grader, is important because it helps their father forget his humiliating job, or convinces their harried mother that she is adequate.

This perpetually organized childhood concept is a recent phenomenon. When I was a child, kids were ignored. The adults had other worries. If we wanted to be in sports, we drove bike in. We never expected our parents to show up. They were too busy. Pity the poor sap whose mother came to every game.

I was left to run wild on spring Saturdays. I cut down trees with a hatchet and built a teepee. I dammed up the drainage ditch, then busted the dam and watched the torrent with a sense of power. I brought home baby birds, mice, rabbits and lizards. All of them died, so I held funerals.

I tore apart a little old gas engine without permission. I smashed the gauges on abandoned cars out back. I played with matches. I tried to kidnap a neighbor kid and hold him for ransom. I sat on the roof on sunny days and used mirrors to blind passersby.

As long as I didn't disrupt the economy, I was ignored. Grandparents, neighbors and parents objected only when the destruction and mayhem interrupted their work. I think most kids from my generation had the same experience.

Earlier generations were even less watched. My dad attached a homemade rocket to his bike and nearly blew himself into eternity. Later, to see if gasoline really does burn, he attached a lit match to a door spring and held it up to the gas nozzle. He squeezed the nozzle, only to have the rush of gasoline put the match out. End of experiment.

Modern parents seem reluctant to let their kids make their own fun and discover things on their own. They didn't learn the wisdom of their parents: let kids be kids. They might get bruised up a bit, but they'll learn.

Riding the Refs

The reason we have an endless stream of interscholastic sports from elementary age on up is that such competition supposedly "builds character."

Perhaps. But many parents and coaches seem far more interested in having a winning record than in building character. Why else would they act like they do? Why else would they yell at the referees, even at elementary school contests?

Sure, referees make mistakes. Sometimes many. But they're paid peanuts if anything at all. They do their best. More important, what a horrible example it sets for children when adults act like whining crybabies.

I remember the last time I yelled at a referee. While home on break from college, I attended a high school wrestling match. It wasn't going well for the home team, and I just knew the referee was at fault. I yelled. I made up nasty insults. People around me thought I was quite funny.

The whistle blew. The match stopped, and the crowd quieted down to hear the latest ruling. As the referee approached the scorer's table, I let fly with a long string of complaints.

The referee, who knew me from my high school glory days as student manager, looked me right in the eye. He wasn't angry. In fact, it looked like he felt sorry for me. He didn't say a word. But the look he gave me said, "you're better than that." That look shut me up that night, and for good. I felt like a fool.

Life isn't fair. It never will be. The sooner people of any age realize that, the better. All we can do is do our best, all of the time, and accept the results, however wrong. Acceptance of life's frequent unfairness is called adulthood.

The perfect place to teach children this important aspect of character is on the athletic floor. The only proper response to a bad break is to get up off the floor and try harder. Former Twins manager Tom Kelly understood this, and was harsh with any player who argued with an umpire.

Unfortunately, not everybody reaches adulthood. Some go through life thinking the world owes them a fair shake. These are the people who whine about their rights, file endless grievances, clog our courts with lawsuits—and yell at referees at high school sporting events.

Americans are known throughout the world for whininess and lawsuits. No other country has so many lawyers per capita. A prominent Australian historian once called American society a "culture of complaint."

It is time to stop this silliness where it starts: In our schools, where children are supposed to be learning character. School boards and administrators should take the lead.

High school coaches who cross the line from discussion to argument with officials should be fired immediately. Who cares how many wins they have. If they set a bad example for the kids, they're gone. Parents who yell at officials should be kicked off the premises.

That'll never happen, of course. But at least the rest of the spectators could turn around and stare at the crybabies. Maybe then the whiners will catch on that they look like fools. Maybe they will, at long last, develop some character.

Gone to State

If you ignore March, it will eventually go away. But March isn't easy to ignore. It throws frequent tantrums just to remind us that we are in the grip of the worst month of the year.

Storms, slush, cold–and funerals! March is a big month for funerals. In fact, I think over half of the funerals I have attended in my life have been in March. People make it through the dark winter months, but March is just too much.

The most common cure for March madness, of course, is to follow the local high school sports team. If tournaments were in any other month, they wouldn't cause such hysteria. But tournaments happen in March for a reason: to give thousands of desperate people a reason to live.

To spread the joy, the Minnesota High School League has divided up schools into about a dozen classes, ranging from A to AAA to AAAAA, each with their own champion. You have to use A's, because nobody wants to be class B, or a C, or especially an F. Losing the Class F final would ruin kids' self-esteem and create dozens of serial killers–thus all the A's.

The hysteria of tournaments so effectively combats March blues that every town in Minnesota will soon demand to "go to state." Their demands will be granted by a special session of the Legislature. It will be a slam-dunk proposal, as popular as those stupid tax refunds.

After all, is it fair to have a bunch of rosy-cheeked adolescents, most of whom don't realize that going to state is a life-or-death matter, destroy the vacation plans of the entire town by losing in double overtime in the region finals?

Mom won't get to load up the credit card at the megamall unless Jeremy and his mates pull off the big victory. Jeremy wants to win, sure, but his real fear is of disappointing Mom. He remembers the pain of her calling him a wimp after the big loss to A-F-M-J-P-R-W Comets last December.

Dad's even worse. He is still smarting from his senior year of high school when his team finished with a 7-14 record. Of course, he missed 10 games due to rules violations, but no mention is made of that. The kids aren't aware that their athletic exploits are his only hope for redemption.

Take a look in the hotel lobbies down in St. Paul during tournaments, and the obvious becomes even more obvious: high school sports are for the parents.

Players walk around in a sullen daze, the weight of the town's pride on their shoulders. They never look like they're having much fun. Adolescence isn't much fun, anyway.

But the parents! Intoxicated by pride, adventure, shopping, and other substances, they practically glow. St. Paul at tourney time is like summer camp all over again, but without the rules.

Yes, a trip to the state tournament remains the single best way to make the year's most miserable month bearable. Go team go.

Awards

The more clubs and organizations lose their vitality, the more likely they are to conjure up awards for their own members, or whoever else will show up to accept one.

Plaques by the dozen, certificates of achievement, of appreciation, of merit, of recognition—the copy machine runs them off until it overheats. The local paper dutifully prints pictures of the smiling recipients of the Very Best Person of the Year award shaking hands with the Grand Poobah.

Everybody seems to think it is rude not to accept an award. And most people enjoy a little notoriety whether it is earned or not. So, nobody ever questions this whole silly awards process. It goes on and on, and the honors multiply faster than tent worms in May.

It begins early. What student can make it through high school without being pelted with awards? I recall getting certificates from clubs I didn't remember joining. In college, I served as vice-president of some society which never met and accomplished nothing whatsoever, but when my term ended I got a nice pin for all of my dedicated hard work. Of course I reveled in the attention.

At the risk of never winning another award, I make the following impolitic suggestion: Isn't it the height of arrogance to hand out awards and expect people to be grateful to receive them?

Most people enjoy getting awards enough to ignore the fact that the organization which gives the award is actually congratulating itself more than anything. Yes, the grand exalted Committee on the Granting of Awards holds it in their power to decide who will be declared the Very Best Person of the Year.

When the Very Best Person of the Year bursts into tears at the podium, when the audience gives the Very Best Person of the Year a standing ovation, and when the picture of the handshake with the Grand Poobah is printed in the paper, the underlying message is: What a grand organization!

Lost in all of this is the sad fact that most organizations do little more than hand out awards. The awards banquet is the central event in their annual cycle. The people who decide the awards are merely poor saps who missed a meeting and were appointed against their will to the awards committee.

The awards scam is a conspiracy which benefits both parties, so it will go on. Occasionally, but very rarely, some crank with an overdeveloped sense of integrity will refuse to accept an award out of a sense that it wasn't earned, or out of a conviction that most organizations which hand out plaques and pins haven't earned the right to bestow such trinkets.

But human vanity loves to be massaged. The most useless organization can announce an award and even a cynical recipient will run out for a new tie, don his best suit, comb his hair, and drive over to the awards banquet for a night of bad food and worse speeches by people for whom he wouldn't cross the street if they weren't holding a plaque with his name on it.

Committees

One of life's great mysteries: How is it that you can take a dozen sensible, bill-paying, responsible, sober, mild-mannered folks, put them together on a committee, and suddenly they become more dangerous than a drunken twenty-one-year-old in a Camaro?

Even a committee of the most decent folks can quickly morph into a many-headed beast. Nothing is safe. Old trees fall to the chain saw. Beautiful buildings crumble. Ugly structures spring up in their place. Antique church fixtures are auctioned off. Bulldozers are turned loose to wreak random destruction.

Committees can create as well as destroy, but their creations are usually limited to a list of infuriating regulations. In the committee environment, silly rules spring up thicker than Canadian thistle on the edge of a manure pile.

In the country, church committees are the usual culprit. In the suburbs, condominium associations take the cake. Committees, boards, associations, consortiums—all should come equipped with day-glow orange warning signs.

Something happens to groups of people who are given power over other people near them. Somehow, they manage as a group to be less intelligent than any one of the group's members. Even an Altar Guild of gray-haired Lutheran ladies can turn into a snakepit of intrigue, plotting and revenge.

Individual people can be reasoned with, but committees and boards seldom respond to anything less convincing than a sledgehammer. Reason means nothing. Good sense disappears. Humanity is elbowed aside by sterile procedure.

In particular, any group that takes it upon itself to issue permits of any sort sends shivers up my spine. It's a good thing I live in the country. The thought of a neighborhood association or a city council telling me to clean up my junk pile is enough to make me start collecting guns.

Nothing beautiful has ever come out of a committee. No committee has ever written an inspiring piece of music, or created a beautiful work of art, or designed a building of lasting merit.

No, the best that can be hoped for of a committee is that they deadlock on every issue so they don't do any damage.

Money matters dominate committees. We can save a few dollars on fuel by blocking out all the windows, so we'd better do it. If we pave the cemetery, we won't have to pay for mowing. All in favor say aye.

It takes great strength of character for a member of a committee to stand up for spending an extra dollar to save something beautiful or old or of sentimental value. So, most committee members stay silent, let the dullards with the calculators hypnotize them with numbers, take a quick vote, and hope to get home in time for the ten o'clock news.

What good things there are in this world exist due to the unleashing of individual genius. Great artists, musicians, composers and writers submit to no judgement of their work but their own and that of a few respected peers. Committees play no role except to grant silly awards after the fact.

Leaders of people have to work through committees, but the great leaders are great in spite of committees. In fact, great leaders often become great leaders because they have an ability to bludgeon, shove, and browbeat the committees in their path into allowing something good to happen.

Such leaders are rare. Between those great leaders, we are stuck with the mediocrity produced by committees of every sort, on every level, everywhere around us.

Gitagadder Lodge

The local post of the Gitagadder Lodge held their spring banquet and annual meeting at the VFW last Tuesday night. Twenty-two members attended. A good time was had by all.

According to custom, Helmer Nelson roasted a pig and Harriet Skordal brought her famous potato salad. Harriet's potato salad is famous not because it tastes good, but because she insists upon bringing a vat of it wherever two or more are gathered. Most of it goes in the garbage, stuck between paper plates, but she never seems to catch on.

After the meal, Gitagadder president Arvid Nelson opened the business meeting. Although not a born leader, Arvid had been so flattered two years ago when he was offered the presidency of Gitagadder only one year after moving to town that he accepted immediately.

Little did he know that the only discernible duty of the president of Gitagadder Lodge is to pick a date for the annual Christmas party which offends nobody, an impossible task.

The issue reared its head at the annual meeting when Ervil Larson announced that he and Elaine wanted to leave for Arizona December 15th this year, and he sure hoped that the Christmas party could be held before then.

Drawing on last year's experience, Arvid said he couldn't pick a date until after the high school sports schedule came out in September. He also knew not to interfere with Advent activities or Monday Night Football.

Last year, the only open date was the Tuesday after Thanksgiving. Nobody said a word in opposition until only seventeen people showed for the party. At the January meeting, Arvid caught heck.

So, Arvid learned the hard way that when the locals stare at you like a herd of drugged holsteins, it doesn't mean that they agree with what you have just said.

Poor Arvid. When he arrived in town to be the new loan officer at the bank, he thought it might be a good idea to join some community organizations. He didn't realize that he was the first new member of Gitagadder in twenty-five years, and that he wasn't entirely welcome. By making him president, the membership got their revenge.

In his first move as president, Arvid proposed a fundraiser to raise the balance in the Gitagadder Ute Scholarship fund above $45.21, where it had been stuck since 1993 when the lodge had allocated $25 to help Jeremy Erickson travel to Australia on a basketball exchange.

No luck. The fundraiser idea died for a lack of a second. Turns out, young Jeremy still hadn't sent a thank you note to Gitagadder. Although they never said a word, the membership felt that if that's the way kids are, they can pay their own way to Australia. So much for the Ute Scholarship Fund.

Next, Arvid suggested that each member canvass ten homes in town in an attempt to reach potential new members. But the stares he got in return were so blank that Arvid knew the idea was doomed.

In despair, Arvid unilaterally appointed a committee of three members to come up with a mission statement. What is Gitagadder about? What is our vision for the future? But month after month went by and the committee never found time to meet. The mission statement idea died a slow death.

Finally, Arvid decided to just show up for the meetings and go through the motions. No new business, no old business, no bright ideas, no discussion.

His popularity soared to a level of begrudging acceptance. Members even shared their opinions on the weather with Arvid over pumpkin bars after meetings.

And so, poor Arvid learned a great truth. Most small-town organizations exist for one reason and one reason alone: lunch. Anything which delays lunch or interferes with its digestion will be resented, resisted, filibustered, and eventually defeated.

New Addresses

After much reportorial legwork, sources have uncovered the founder of the new 911 address system recently imposed upon rural areas, the system whereby an old farmhouse on a mud road at RR 1, Box 126, has been transformed into a suburban estate at 44502 520th Ave. SW.

Ralph L. Twinkledoofer, a career desk clerk at the State Department of Bureaucracy Department in St. Paul, first made a name for himself in the bureaucratic community when he succeeded in requiring farm people to cover their garbage pits and install metal dumpsters instead.

The 911 address system, however, was Twinkledoofer's crowning achievement. With one brilliant stroke, Twinkledoofer accomplished the bureaucrat's dream: he complicated the life of millions for no apparent reason, and with little opposition.

In a rare interview, the recently retired Twinkledoofer revealed what many have long suspected: the installation of the 911 addressing system was all a big practical joke.

"I never thought it would go anywhere," Twinkledoofer said, sounding surprised by his success. "Giving street names to every gravel road in Minnesota was such an obviously ridiculous idea that I was sure it would be laughed out of the legislature."

That was before Twinkledoofer hit upon the brilliant idea of naming his system, "The 911 Address System." Once the powers-that-be were convinced that 44502 520th Ave. SW would somehow be easier for ambulance crews to find than a rural route address, all opposition to the bizarre plan crumbled.

"I can't believe they fell for that one," Twinkledoofer said, somewhat bemused. "I guess if you want to get something silly imposed upon people, you just have to threaten their health."

In retirement, an unrepentant Twinkledoofer collects stories of the mayhem unleashed by his pet project. Stories of people who can't remember their own address. Stories of UPS drivers lost for days. Stories of confused ambulance crews administering CPR to farmers who thought they felt fine.

Twinkledoofer is the first to point out that his success was not complete. His attempt to force high school students to memorize their new addresses in order to graduate failed. "If only I had stuck with four-digit numbers instead of five," he said with a shake of the head, "it probably would have been included in the Profile of Learning."

But that small failure does little to dim Twinkledoofer's dazzling bureaucratic success story. "I never dreamed that I could force every rural resident to order new check blanks," he said with obvious satisfaction.

To make it clear that he was kidding, Twinkledoofer added many whimsical twists to his addressing system. For example, some gravel roads are an avenue if you live on one side and a street if you live on the other.

With a touch of humor, Twinkledoofer decreed that the streets and avenues in a great swath of rural northwestern Minnesota be numbered from the middle of the tiny town of St. Hilaire.

"I can just see out-of-state visitors counting down from 540th Avenue to 320th Avenue, thinking they'll find skyscrapers when they finally get to the single digits," Twinkledoofer said with a chuckle. "Instead, they find themselves at the liquor store in downtown St. Hilaire."

Active in retirement, Twinkledoofer spends his days watching his neighbors to make sure they don't violate city ordinances. "I turned in Mervyn Larson for a noise violation last Thursday," he said with pride, adding that he is working on getting an injunction to force the Bjorkland's down the street to spray for dandelions.

Budget Cuts

With budget cuts looming and tolerance for tax increases low, Mayor Selmer Borseth of Podunk, MN, pop. 732, has put out a call for volunteers to mow the lawn around the fire hall.

The fire hall doubles as the city council chambers and contains a small corner office for the city clerk. The exterior is painted lime green. Letters cut from plywood and painted pink spell out "Podunk, A City On The Move" on the wall outside the entrance.

In the past, the fire hall lawn was mowed by high school kids hired for the summer, the same ones they hired to wash out the wastebaskets at the school. There were usually six of them, and because washing wastebaskets and mowing the lawn were their only duties, the job eventually got done.

But funding for the Disheveled and Disadvantaged Youth Summer Employment Program was cut by the legislature last session. As a result, keeping the lawn mowed would require a tax hike, which would mean a referendum and maybe a bond levy, and nobody has the initiative for that.

Mayor Borseth and the city council agree that Podunk's hard-earned reputation as a progressive community requires that the lawn outside the chambers of government be kept below knee-level. But they don't care to do it themselves.

What about city maintenance man Earl Poduski? Can't he do it? Well, Earl's too smart for that. In his twenty-seventh year of working for the city, Earl knows better than to take on anything new.

Earl knows that if you take on something new, people will think you mustn't have been busy enough before. If they get the idea that all you do is drink coffee and smoke cigarettes, they'll start piling on projects until you don't have any time to drink coffee and smoke cigarettes.

Earl keeps his job description, which was carefully developed over the course of 17 contentious city council meetings in the late 1980s, in his shirt pocket. Wouldn't you know, there's nothing in there about mowing the lawn around the fire hall.

So, with the weeds growing high, Mayor Borseth put out his call for volunteers. Response was light. In fact, there was none.

It's difficult to imagine what the mayor was thinking. After all, Podunk's churches can't even get their parishioners to mow the cemetery anymore, much less drop enough into the offering plate to hire it done.

If churches can't guilt people into doing something for nothing, City Hall can't expect to do much better. Who in their right mind would rally to the cause of the entity which sends out the water bill? No, the mayor was off in la-la land when he came up with that one.

So, it looks like City Clerk Jenna Henderson will have to prod her husband Joe out of the bar long enough to push the mower around the fire hall a few times. That is, if she doesn't want sweet clover to overtake her workplace.

Joe's on permanent disability due to a back injury–but he can still mow, particularly if there's a six-pack involved.

And, who knows, mowing the lawn at the fire hall might give Joe a sense of purpose. He might take pride in the place. People might see a transformation in Joe and pass the hat to reward him for his nice work.

Yes, spurred by budget cuts, a new spirit of volunteerism just might sweep through Podunk and across the country. Pass the hat, people! Just don't call it a tax.

Gas Stations

Most progress is anything but progress, but the improvement in small town gas stations in the past decade or two has been a change for the better.

If you had told me ten years ago that the time would come when I could purchase a cappuccino at our local gas station, I would have said you were nuts. But now I take it for granted that every little gas station in every small town will have a convenience store with goodies galore.

Gone are the dark and dirty filling stations of old. The dusty, oil-soaked concrete floors which sweeping could not improve have been replaced by brightly-lit tile.

No more cracked vinyl chairs and overflowing ashtrays on either side of the front door where old men sit for hours and leer at any female who dares enter.

Ah, the wonders of capitalism! Somebody finally figured out that women buy gas, too, and that women will likely go where they feel comfortable. So, the leering old men were removed—not by force, but by eliminating their natural habitat of cracked-vinyl chairs and overflowing ashtrays.

Also missing from today's gas station: girlie calendars, dust-covered cigarette machines, fan belts hanging on the wall above the till, and the smell of oil, gas, anti-freeze, WD-40, all mixed. Most stations have moved their shop way out back so you can no longer hear the *phfffft* of the air wrench, or the screech of a hubcap getting pried off.

There are no grease-covered attendants at gas stations

anymore. The clerks are pressed and clean, likely because they no longer fill your tank for you, wash your windows, check your oil, anything. They're too busy selling lottery tickets or renting movies.

Small town gas stations still can be a social center, but if you don't feel like going in to gab with the locals you can opt out by paying with your credit card at the pump. Pay-at-the-pump is one technology which actually makes life simpler, not more difficult. Imagine that.

And milk. What a great thing to be able to grab a half-gallon of 2% after filling gas, instead of having to weave down the aisles of the grocery store only to pick up six items on sale that you didn't need.

Some gas stations even sell fresh pizza and sub sandwiches. Locals dine at the gas station more frequently than they care to admit. Most towns of less than 1,000 population have never had a pizza joint. A filling station with a pizza place in the back corner constitutes the biggest jump in the small-town quality of life index since cable television.

I can't imagine that many people miss the old-style filling station, with its smoky haze, lecherous ambiance, grumbling, gossip, bad politics, debauched jokes and rock-hard candy bars. Pizza, chips, movies, and fancy coffee are much better.

Small town gas stations, unlike most small town businesses, have entered an era of prosperity something like the drug stores enjoyed back before soda fountains went out. A glistening gas station brightens up what is left of main street, and gives many rural small towns at least one prosperous business to brag about other than the fancy new funeral home.

Nursing Home

About once per year they call from the local nursing home to have me come in and do some music.

They get the same old tunes every year. The residents don't seem to mind, but I think the staff notices. I once slipped in a different song. After I finished, somebody at the nurse's station piped up, "You learned a new one!" She sounded more amazed than excited.

I think I know why it is so difficult for people to visit a nursing home. The place will make you think. Each visit to the nursing home runs around in my head for a couple of days afterwards. Some of the thoughts are tough to shake.

It is always a jolt to see people there whose health must have declined just in the last months, people I know very well I saw gabbing at the coffee shop or mowing their yards last summer.

There is the sadness of watching those whose minds have failed them in the cruelest way: not only have they lost their memory, but they are constantly agitated and unhappy, wanting to go home, wanting to go to the store, wanting to be somewhere else. There is no comforting them.

But, as some philosopher once wrote, where there is suffering there is also joy. One comes with the other. A nursing home is a rich example of this rule.

When Grandpa was in the home, he sat at the dinner table with three other old Scandinavians. In their prime, these four probably would have greeted each other with little more than a gruff hello. However, in their dotage, Grandpa helped cut Clarence's pork chops and Oscar would guide blind old Pete's hands over to his water glass. Kind of touching, I thought.

I'll never forget when one formerly prim and proper Lutheran Sunday school teacher went off on a loud monologue about her fondness for whiskey. "I used to hide it in the back of the fridge," she said, "but now I don't care who finds out!"

People with slight dementia sometimes have a better sense of humor than people with all of their marbles. Like one dignified woman who tended to wander off and eventually had to wear one of those beepers on her ankle. She didn't mind. "This," she told me with as much pride and pomposity as she could muster, "is my medallion."

For my part, I enjoy playing an old hymn like "What a Friend We Have in Jesus" at the home. If I play softly enough, I can hear a solid chorus humming along. The old people know all of the good old melodies.

Once as I played a favorite hymn I caught the eyes of a former school teacher whose stern demeanor used to frighten me. But now she smiled kindly at me and sang along. She knew the words to all four verses, which didn't surprise me.

I was surprised, however, when I tried to talk to her afterwards. I thanked her for singing along, but she looked up at me blankly. It turns out she could no longer speak. She seemed completely out of it, which made it all the more wonderful that we had connected during the hymn.

Nursing homes can be depressing. They remind us of our mortality, and we don't like that. Nobody wants to end up there. Yet, where else can one see little miracles like these?

CHAPTER TWO

ON THE ROAD

Rules of the Road

With all the road washouts due to the recent torrents of rain, getting around our area has become a challenge. Detours of 40 or 50 miles are common, if you can figure out the signs.

Twice I have gotten so lost that I accidentally wormed my way miles behind the detour signs and made it right up to the actual problem. Nice for sightseeing, terrible for making it anywhere on time.

My problems are minor compared to people who have lost homes, businesses, or even those who have to drive fifteen miles to get to town for milk where they used to drive two or three.

But alas, when adversity strikes, the human spirit so often shines through. People help people. Volunteers sandbag. Sympathizers drive for miles to gawk sympathetically. Troops appear with big green trucks. Grief counselors materialize to assist disaster victims in their quest for healing and closure.

Once things settle down, the federal government pulls out its enormous checkbook and starts throwing around the millions. Such generosity! It's as if Grandpa Roosevelt were still alive. Some disaster dollars end up in good places, others end up in funny places, but hey, don't complain.

This last flood brought about a small incident which stirred me to philosophize. As I went north on US Highway 59, I came upon a place where the highway was underwater. Only one lane of the road was open for travel, and the sign said simply: "take turns."

How nice, I thought. Just like the schoolyard. The cars were behaving perfectly. Two would ease slowly through the water going north, then two would go south. It was all very orderly. There were long lines on either side, but nobody seemed to mind. Nobody in any sort of uniform was there to enforce the rules.

Just when I had reached the front of the line and was about to take my turn, a white Jeep Land Rover jumped the line, roared past fifteen cars, and splashed headlong through the water at a high speed.

What a jerk! One bad apple, and the whole system broke down. Now it was every man for himself. Instead of two cars taking their turn from the other way, four decided to pull through. When I pulled out, five or six cars followed. It was chaos.

The incident disturbed me for an hour. Here we had people acting mannerly and orderly without being forced by the law, or by the authorities, to behave. A simple sign, "take turns," was all that was needed.

But one jerk ruined this beautiful example of human beings living together in harmony. Who knows when and how order was restored.

As the miles wore on, I decided I was being a little hard on the people in the Land Rover. Perhaps they had a medical emergency, or maybe they were late for a funeral.

But right then, I pulled up behind that same white Land Rover. It was making a left turn, and not into a hospital parking lot. No, the Land Rover was hellbent for the casino. Emergency, indeed!

Childhood Vacations

The buttery sunshine of hot July evenings brings back memories of childhood vacations, when Mom and Dad would load us up in the LTD station wagon and head west for our annual trip.

Hundreds of mental snapshots: of the tame chipmunks at the top of the gondola ride in Estes Park, CO. Of the Clark's nutcracker birds which snatched peanuts out of our hands when we stopped along that wild road over Bear Tooth Pass. Of the huge goldfish in the river in Hot Springs, SD.

I recall hiking between the rust-colored spires of Bryce Canyon when I was missing both my front teeth. There was the time the air conditioning on the LTD went out in Flagstaff, AZ in July. Or the time I went underwater without my nose plugged for the first time in a Ramada Inn pool in Eugene, OR.

There weren't a lot of chain motels in the 1970s, so you had to be careful. Mom and Dad insisted upon checking if the room smelled bad before they checked in. They turned down as many rooms as they took, which embarrassed me horribly.

Twenty-five dollars was acceptable, $32 a splurge. A pool was an exciting bonus, but many of them were ice-cold and unusable. I didn't like to swim, anyway.

A bigger treat than the pool was the television in the room. We didn't have television at home, so motels were where we made up for lost time. As the sun set over the mountains outside, our family huddled in a dark room around a TV watching an old black and white movie.

Motels back then could be pretty rough, but every now and then we would hit the jackpot, as we did in Lincoln City, OR in 1976. Our room, which cost $22, was actually a suite of rooms spread over two stories with an enormous picture window overlooking the Pacific Ocean fifty feet below.

The best memory of that stay? Watching Mark Fidrych of the Detroit Tigers pitch against the Red Sox on ABC's "Monday Night Baseball." Howard Cosell announced. I suspect the ocean surf roared in the background, but I don't recall.

"Candid Camera" was a family favorite, and "The Carol Burnett Show" made Mom laugh until she cried. In Burns, OR at Uncle Don and Aunt Lois's ranch, Billy Martin and Reggie Jackson got in a fight in the dugout on NBC's "Game of the Week" from Fenway Park. Unforgettable. I think we also rode horses that visit, but I am not sure.

Never forget the time in beautiful Fort Collins, CO, when my sister and I managed to watch twenty minutes of the racy 1970s show "Soap" before Mom realized what was going on and put a stop to it.

Glacier Park, Montana, 1977. No television, but I managed to get a dim radio signal of the Twins playing the expansion Seattle Mariners. It was a Seattle station. The Twins won behind the pitching of Geoff Zahn. I spent two hours sitting in the car, fine tuning the radio, sitting in different positions to make the signal come in better.

Yes, great memories of getting away from it all, refreshing one's soul, and experiencing nature's wonders.

Driving Crazy

En route to Tucson, AZ from Minnesota, one travels hundreds of miles of lonely nothingness across South Dakota, Nebraska, Kansas and the panhandles of Oklahoma and Texas. The scenery finally gets interesting midway through New Mexico.

The hazards of long, lonely highways go beyond the danger of falling asleep at the wheel. The worst thing about such long trips is that there is nothing to do while driving but think.

I am okay on the road as long as I daydream of being President and solving the Mideast crisis, or of pitching shut-outs for the Twins, or of finding oil reserves on my land in Minnesota—all equally improbable scenarios.

But take a wrong turn down memory lane and pretty soon you can be reliving that time you got beat up in eighth grade and oh, how you wish you could have a crack at that guy now. Or the time your athletic ability was insulted by the gym teacher. Boy, I'll give him an earful if I see him at the mall.

Old embarrassments return to life. The time I forgot my lines for the play. The time I went to school with a rip in my pants. The time I forgot to show up for a final exam in college. The time I accidentally rushed into the women's bathroom at the Country Kitchen.

Even if you manage to purge your sordid past from your head, something else will likely creep in.

Isn't that little lump behind my ear getting bigger? I

should have it checked. Or maybe I shouldn't. I can just imagine what they'll find. Probably a brain tumor.

Twenty miles down that hypochondriac road and you're picking out hymns for your funeral, to which nobody will come because you've wasted your life doing things like driving to Tucson.

Just then some jerk cuts in front of you and forces you to slam on your brakes. That jolts you back to reality, but then you spend the next fifty miles plotting revenge on him. Man, if I was only driving a dented old wreck, I'd ram him and his fat Cadillac into the next ravine.

Time to try the radio, but that does no good. The preachers on rural Texas radio stations rant and rave up and down the dial. The signal for *All Things Considered* fades in and out from the nearest college town.

So, I am learning a new technique to keep my mind calm on long trips. It is called: look at the scenery. I try to find something interesting in all scenery, even in the dull states. For example, a while back I noticed that none of the ponds in Indiana have cattails.

Now, why do Indiana ponds have sleek, weed-free shores instead of the masses of impenetrable reeds which border our swamps in Minnesota? I spent about sixty miles pondering that one. If anybody has an idea, let me know.

Today, I discovered that there are oil wells in southwest Kansas. In fact, oil wells are about the only interesting feature of southwest Kansas. Some pump so slowly you have to watch them for a minute to detect movement.

But at least watching them pump gives one something to do on the road besides think.

Amarillo till Morning

Greetings from Amarillo, Texas. With the weather forecast looking foul at home, and with Christmas obligations out of the way, I jumped in my pickup and headed south in search of sunshine and warmth.

Instead, I ran into snow and ice on the Texas panhandle. Not so bad, but these people aren't used to winter driving. They race along like nothing's wrong–until the first pile-up. Then they slow to a crawl–until they forget that first pile-up and speed up into the next pile-up.

Four pile-ups today on I-40, one bad enough so I had to back up to the most recent exit to get past the mess.

Exhausted of it all, I pulled into Amarillo. A banner outside the Super 8 announced a special deal, a double room for $35.99. Good deal, I thought, a single room couldn't be any more than that.

No such luck. The clerk, clearly not one of Amarillo's finest, said a single room would be $42.99. I asked about the special. Did I have to find another person to get the reduced rate?

"Those are for double smoking rooms out back. Nobody wants those," he said, annoyed that I expected the promotional banner to bear any relation to reality.

Annoyed enough, apparently, to put me in room 123. Room 123 has two doors, he explained. If the inside one doesn't work, try the outside one, it should work. The room should be clean, he added.

The door worked and the room had been cleaned, but once inside, I saw that the room had no window. Stupid me, I had never thought to ask for a room with a window.

I wasn't about to spend the rest of this miserable day in a cave. I went back to the front desk and asked Mr. Friendly for a room with a window. He tossed me the key for room 131 without saying a word.

Room 131 was fine. I settled in and settled down for a nap. But just as I started to drift off, I heard a key in the keyhole. I jumped up, ran to the door, opened it to find a very surprised older couple wondering what I was doing in the room they had rented.

Apparently there was some demand for a room with a window. Mr. Friendly had also checked the older couple into room 131. I told them I regretted that I didn't have an extra bed and sent them back to the front desk.

To relax, I decided to drive to the Barnes & Noble and spend the evening reading. It was icy. I got lost twice on the way. Ambulances and fire trucks roared to and fro, but nothing was going to stop me from getting to Barnes & Noble.

I stopped for directions until I finally found the place. The bookstore sign was a sight for sore eyes, almost as welcome as the lights of home.

But I had forgotten. It was snowing, and this is Texas. The Barnes & Noble, like everything else, had closed due to the weather.

Colorado Driving

I-70 across Colorado from west to east looks harmless enough on the map. A few bends, but nothing out of the ordinary. It's interstate, after all, it couldn't be too bad, I thought.

Yeah, right. The road was dry, the sky was clear, but I-70 was anything but easy. Twisting, winding, climbing up and down, the freeway clings to cliffs, tunnels through mountains, and shoots down canyons.

I-70 clears two major mountain passes—one at Vail, CO which is at 10,000 feet elevation, and a second at Loveland which is over 11,000 ft. My ears popped on the way up. When I stopped to stretch and have a look around at the mountains, I got woozy from the thin air.

It seems strange to have such high mountain passes open in January, until you remember that on the opposite side of those passes from Denver are the big ski resorts. Vail. Aspen. Breckenridge. Copper Mountain.

The CEOs and movie stars who own $2.1 million condominiums in Vail aren't going to be too happy if they can't get their Mercedes across the mountain pass. For that reason, I suspect that I-70 is one of the best maintained, most frequently-plowed stretches of highway on this earth.

What made I-70 so unnerving to me was not the curves so much as it was the 75-mile-per hour speed limit and the dozens of Audis, Volvos, Jaguars and SUVs whose owners insisted upon driving 80 miles-per-hour, curves or none.

I held it down to 65 miles-per-hour, hoping to catch some scenery and stay alive. My slow pace inspired the luxury car owners to use sign language as they sped past. One even took both hands off the wheel to angrily flash the numbers seven and five at me several times.

Yes, some pretty happy people up there at Vail trying to spend their millions!

From Loveland Pass, the highway drops six thousand feet down to Denver in just a few miles. Quite a ride, tough on the brakes.

Big yellow highway signs warned truckers of the steep grades in unusually informal and urgent language: "You aren't at the bottom yet!" "Don't be fooled, there's more to come!"

I wasn't fooled. As I careened down the canyon, I felt like a pinball bouncing off the bonus bumpers, shooting through the extra-ball chute.

Finally, the road swooped into Denver. I didn't even stop for coffee. I pretended I had gained momentum from the big hill, and sped straight on through to Nebraska.

As much as I enjoy the mountain scenery, there is something about returning to the Great Plains that causes one to breath a sigh of relief. Some of the relief comes from the lack of hills and curves, I am sure.

But it is also good to see barns, windbreaks, fields and farmhouses again, and know you are once again at the tender mercies of the good people who live amongst them.

Colorado Plateau

To alleviate the pain of leaving Arizona, I took a new route home. From Flagstaff, I drove north on two-lane roads across the desolate reaches of the great Colorado Plateau.

Flagstaff itself is a snowy resort and college town at 7,000 feet elevation. On the city's north side is lonely Humphery's Peak. Trains rumble through town all night. Lying in the hotel room bed, you hear each whistle twice: first the toot from the train, then the echo off the mountain, clear as a bell, in a different key.

As the sun rose on a perfectly clear morning following two days of snow, I scooted around the base of Humphery's Peak and headed due north across the wasteland. The mountain remained in my rearview mirror for an hour, until it was merely a white pimple on the plateau.

I skipped the Grand Canyon, saving twenty dollars. An impressive hole in the ground, but what do you do once you've looked over the edge?

Unless you bring a mule, all you can do is drive to another spot, find a place to park, get out, and look over the edge again. A few minutes later you're in the gift shop looking over souvenir spoons for Aunt Ethel.

I prefer scenery you can drive through, and I was astounded by the relentlessly spectacular six hundred miles of back country between Flagstaff and Denver.

Cliffs, mesas, pillars, arches, canyons. Layer after layer of rock eroded by the eons into every formation imaginable.

Red cliffs, orange cliffs, gently rounded sandstone hills with pink and green layers. Every turn in the road brought a new combination of color and formation—all of it, on this day, frosted in fresh snow.

Monument Valley is an open space, almost like the Red River Valley. But in the middle of the vast plain stand about a half a dozen vertical rock formations, like tree stumps, each a thousand feet tall. It was an eerie scene, like a graveyard, but on such a large scale that I felt like I was on Jupiter.

A few miles later a sign pointed to the Valley of the Gods. In the distance I saw a forest of spectacular layered orange pillars on yet another flat plain. I pulled over so I could gawk without rolling my pickup into a canyon.

Photographers by the thousands attempt to capture the grandeur of this astounding landscape. The resulting coffee table books are nice enough, but none of them captures the dignity of the place, the haunted loneliness, the enchantment.

There is something about enormous rocks that conjures up majestic, dignified, serious thoughts. The formations confront you with geological time. Not only did the layers have to build up, but then they wore down into mountains, pillars and cliffs. This all happened well before I was born.

The previous day, I had driven through Phoenix. I traveled sixty miles of freeway without seeing one inch of ground that wasn't either covered in concrete or manicured by some landscape company. The skies were dark with pollution. Traffic was thick. Most of that mess happened after I was born.

Those sixty miles in Phoenix exhausted me in every sense, but the six hundred mile drive on two-lane across the Colorado Plateau invigorated me competely. Those big old rocks and wide spaces forced me into a broader perspective, and that is always a good thing.

Airport Security

Had my first chance to endure the tightened airport security measures last weekend. Getting through security isn't too bad unless your belt buckle makes the beeper go, or unless your name gets pulled for the random security check.

If you set off the beeper or get spit out by the computer, you have to step aside and be "hand-wanded" while another guard empties out your carry-on bags and rifles through your things.

But I had no worries. Turns out, the security check isn't random at all. The only ones who get pulled aside for security checks are old ladies with white hair.

The government has denied that they are picking on senior women, insisting that they do not single out people with a particular age or gender profile. But it is common knowledge in airports these days that if you have a gray beehive hairdo, you better get ready for a thorough public hand-wanding.

Most of the grannies I saw took the invasion of privacy in good humor. In the Reno airport, a lady from New York stood with her arms outstretched as the diligent security guard ran the hand wand up and down her body. Ten feet away, the lady's little suitcase was emptied on a table for all to see.

The hand-wand beeped. The security guard ran the hand-wand all over the area which produced the beep. Beep, beep, beep. The guard zeroed in on the carpet knife, or whatever it was that this suspicious-looking grandma had tucked away.

The woman rolled her eyes heavenward, determined to endure the humiliation with the stoicism of Joan of Arc. But the guard persisted with the hand-wand until the woman finally closed her eyes, gritted her teeth, and confessed, "there is a metal buckle on my bra strap."

Satisfied that the woman wasn't wired with explosives, the guard let her put on her shoes and move through. "They should just make us show up in those hospital gowns," she mumbled. "I haven't been hand-wanded like that in sixty years."

The security guards, to their credit, maintain good humor, and do their best to comfort their victims. They are, after all, just obeying orders from Washington. If my trip was any indication, those orders are to put a good scare in the nation's old ladies, especially if they sport a hairdo that looks like a turban.

Of course, great-grandmothers have never hesitated to use terrorism, but they usually limit it to the "you never visit, you never call" variety. Now, apparently, they have become a threat to our nation's security. With people on edge, this is no time to fool around.

My confidence in our airline security system grew when I saw how thoroughly they are searching and hand-wanding elderly women. I have always thought that bunch was up to no good. Now at least I know they are being watched.

Of course, no system is fool-proof. You know that somewhere, sometime, some grandma will get through security strapped to the nines with explosives, eager to strike a blow against American imperialism on her way to see the grandkids in Seattle.

Great Lakes

The main problem driving from the Upper Midwest to the East Coast is getting around the Great Lakes. The most direct route is to drive south of them all, but that means fighting through the drag-race traffic and frequent toll booths of Chicago. This trip, I decided to weave between the big lakes instead.

The longer, more remote northern route features endless woods, frequent swamps and long stretches of lonely two-lane highway. All the way from Bagley, MN to Buffalo, NY, the golden tamarack trees glowed, their falling needles dusting the road with bright yellow.

The wilderness, the empty highways, the small towns and the forests are a wonderful alternative to the freeways and big cities on the southern route. But it was close brushes with the lakes themselves that made the trip most memorable.

My motel room in Ashland, WI was fifty feet from the shore of Lake Superior. The sullen gray waters beneath the bruised clouds reminded me of a phrase sung by Gordon Lightfoot: "Superior, they said, never gives up her dead, when the skies of November turn gloomy." I was glad not to be out on the water in an ore boat.

US Highway 2 hugs the northern shore of Lake Michigan for over 100 miles. Huge waves broke against the shore. When the road dipped down near the beach, gusts of wind pelted my pickup with a mixture of sand and spray.

Highway 2 is mostly two lane, but almost every mile of

it from Duluth to Mackinac is newly paved. I got so carried away driving like a Gran Prix driver on the smooth curves that when "low fuel" light came on, I discovered I was thirty-nine miles from the next town. I made it, but the stress of driving on empty in the middle of nowhere took several months off of my life expectancy.

Big bodies of water mean big bridges. All told, I crossed five enormous high bridges between Duluth and Buffalo. The most impressive was the Mackinac suspension bridge connecting Upper and Lower Michigan. Far below churned the strait connecting Lake Michigan with Lake Huron.

For one hour I was stuck on the high bridge from Port Huron, MI into Canada, waiting to go through customs. In the channel way below, the cold waters swirled from Lake Erie to the right into Lake Huron on the left.

The bridge which crossed high above the harbor in Hamilton, Ontario was the most frightening. It seemed old and unsafe. A forty mile-per-hour wind pushed my pickup from side to side. Three feet from my left tires, the pavement abruptly ended. No curb, no barrier–just the abyss.

The final crossing of my trip was over the bridge at Niagara Falls, where the waters from Lake Erie tumble down into Lake Ontario. If you can block out from your mind all the various viewing platforms and towers, as well as the cluster of hotels on both the Canadian and American side of the falls, Niagara is everything you could imagine.

Niagara Falls was the crowning jewel of a three-day journey between the five biggest lakes in the world. I've seen the Great Lakes on the map since I was in elementary school, but until I saw them up close, their utter immensity didn't hit home.

Hotel Bargain

If you have a credit card and access to the Internet, you can place a bid on most anything. Baseball cards, used cars, paintings, clothing, airline tickets, grand pianos, toilet paper, you name it.

The only item I have bid on over the web is a hotel room. Last winter, I placed a lowball bid on a room in a luxury hotel and got it for less than what even the budget motels charge. Last week I was in need of a vacation, so I decided to try my luck on a hotel room in downtown Minneapolis.

The game works like this: you set the dates, your preferred level of luxury, the general area where you wish to stay, and your price. Within seconds, the gnomes of the Internet dangle your offer in front of several hotels.

In fewer than fifteen minutes, you are informed whether your bid was accepted, and by which hotel. The hotel which accepts your bid immediately charges your credit card, no refunds allowed.

This time, my first two bids were turned down. Must be a big convention in Minneapolis, I decided. Instead of limiting myself to downtown, I decided to widen my net to include the Metrodome and University neighborhood.

Bingo! My offer was accepted. For less than half regular price, I had landed a room at a Sheraton, which the gnomes claimed was near the Metrodome. I jumped in my pickup and headed to the big city, durn proud of my dealin' smarts.

Upon my arrival, it was painfully obvious why this particular Sheraton accepts low bids from ignorant hicks. The hotel wasn't near anything.

No restaurants. No shops. No parks, nothing. The Metrodome was four miles away.

No, this Sheraton was smack dab in the middle of an industrial park in northeast Minneapolis. The hotel was a lonely island in a sea of warehouses, trucking firms, chemical companies and other enormous gravel-roofed buildings surrounded by acres of asphalt.

The hotel took the low bid on the room, but you should see their prices for everything else. Local calls? Two dollars each. Breakfast? Eight bucks, minimum. I didn't turn on the TV for fear of going broke.

To show their contempt for Internet bargain hunters, the hotel staff stuck me in a room right next to the banquet hall—just where you don't want to be on a Saturday night. Boom, boom, boom, a wedding dance pounded away until 1 a.m.

And yes, there was a convention going on in Minneapolis, a 1950s car gathering at the state fairgrounds. Ten thousand cars in all, about 100 of which were in the parking lot of my hotel. I spent part of the evening eavesdropping on the spit-polishing codgers who had driven the gaudy cars in from all over the country.

It wasn't long before I got my fill of chrome, fins, hair grease and big talk. I took a walk. Because it was the weekend, the streets of the industrial park were utterly abandoned. In two miles I encountered two cars and no pedestrians. It was blissfully quiet.

In fact, if it hadn't been for the chain link fence and barbed wire, it would have felt much like walking on a lonely township road back home.

Red River Valley

During the past few weeks I have had several occasions to traverse the vast depopulated expanse of the Red River Valley, from top to bottom and side to side. We who live here forget that the Valley is one of the world's unique natural features.

A table-top flat lake bottom with rich, black soil is completely unusual. In fact, the only place in the world similar to the Valley that I can think of are the plains of Poland and the Ukraine.

They grow the same crops in the black soil of the Ukraine as we do in ours. But their massive plains aren't table-top flat like the Red River Valley, and there are more trees, villages, and roads in Eastern Europe than there are here.

Although the cities of Fargo and Grand Forks have grown in recent years, I suspect that the rural areas of the Red River Valley have less than one tenth the population they did at their peak just before the war.

Josef Stalin killed or starved out three million Ukrainian farmers in order to establish more efficient communal farms of thousands of acres. In the Red River Valley, the same stark efficiency was attained bloodlessly through market forces.

Despite the loss of most of its population, there is little visible desolation in the Valley. The old buildings are generally torn down. The few left standing add a rustic touch, and there aren't enough of them to make the place look messy.

In fact, my impression is that the Valley looks streamlined

and clean. I can't imagine what the place was like in the 1940s when there were ten times the number of farms, and when they farmed those big fields with B Allis Chalmers and John Deere putt-putts.

One thing missing in the Red River Valley–and I am probably the only one who misses it–is a big cathedral. I'll never forget traveling on a train through a wheat-growing plain north of Cambridge, England. In the distance loomed the massive Ely cathedral–taller than any water tower, larger than any grain elevator, towering over a town of 900.

What a sight. And to think they built the thing in the 1400s. As I entered the cathedral door I heard echoes of the choir practicing. Later, the huge pipe organ roared to life. High overhead, the streams of sunshine played through the pillars and the stain glass windows.

We don't have cathedrals of that sort in the Valley. Just a few big grain terminals, none of which have pipe organs or choirs.

Since that day in Ely, I have had the completely nutty dream of building a cathedral in the Red River Valley. I'd put it out west of Halstad, visible from I-29, smack dab in the middle of a sugar beet field.

This project would cost $50 million or so to realize, I suppose. I haven't talked to an architect. Prospects for public funding are poor. But my Cathedral of the Prairie gives me something to daydream about as I trundle along the Valley's lonely back roads.

Thanksgiving in Indiana

Spent Thanksgiving on the banks of the Ohio River in southern Indiana. I was on important business: an uncle who lives down there needed a wood stove from up here delivered down there.

Of course the stove could have easily been shipped. But one can't let an excuse to travel slip by, especially a chance to see a new part of the country and meet new people.

The stove in question was one of those external jobbies, a tin hut with a chimney sticking up. With that thing in the box, my pickup looked like something out of the Beverly Hillbillies. Boy, was I popular on the interstate. People stared, waved and laughed.

One couple followed me into a rest area to settle a bet. The woman approached the pickup. "What is it?" she said. When I said it was a wood stove, she let out a whoop.

Her husband had bet that it was an outhouse. The kids were sure that it was a playhouse. But the woman had correctly guessed that it was a wood stove. She ran back to their car before I could even ask what she had won.

Some redneck at a gas station in southern Illinois asked me what the heck that thing was. I tried to convince him that I had a wood burning pickup, one of the first off the assembly line. He didn't fall for it, probably because I had a gas nozzle in my tank at the time.

By the end of the 1,000 mile trip the novelty had worn off, and I was eager to shed the 1,000 extra pounds so I could quit driving like an old lady.

After the forklift removed the stove from my pickup, I sat down with my uncle's in-laws for an Indiana Thanksgiving dinner. It was even more excessive than a Minnesota Thanksgiving dinner, and every bit as scrumptious.

The only real surprise was oyster dressing. As far as I can tell, it is just regular dressing with some oysters thrown in. Delicious, much better than lutefisk, but I suspect it is a tradition that won't catch on north of Des Moines.

Another new thing to me: the turkey was deep fried outside in a big vat over a flame, not baked in the oven.

There were six pies for twelve people. Two pecan pies, two pumpkin, one apple, and, much to my surprise and consternation, one gooseberry pie. Fortunately, the two gooseberry pie fanatics present split the pie between them, thus saving me the guilt of having to turn it down.

Oh, and one other difference from a typical Minnesota Thanksgiving. It was so warm that we ate outside in the shop. As the sun set, a chill did set in, and the new wood stove wasn't hooked up yet.

To offset the cold, somebody broke out a bottle of high-octane homemade wine decanted in an old Jim Beam bottle. I am telling you, that stuff warmed me up every bit as good as if that wood stove had been hooked up and ready to go.

Baseball Trip

While surfing the internet, I came across a summer vacation idea I couldn't resist: A bus tour of eight major league ballparks in nine days. Eight cities, fourteen teams—with all tickets, hotels and transportation arranged ahead of time.

Things change. Last year at this time, I took off to Europe with a backpack and very few plans. I was full of romantic notions of wandering around, staying where the spirit led, meeting new people, going with the flow.

Well, I spent the first night of my free-spirited adventure on a cot in a boarding house in Cambridge, England. The tiny, stinky room had apparently housed a shedding sheep dog for the previous month. Hair everywhere. No air conditioning. The only bathroom was two floors down.

I had forgotten that I was thirty-eight years old. My hippie days were long behind me. In fact, don't think they ever happened. In any case, I learned that I had grown too old to get along without running water, a nice bed, and hot meals.

Last year at this time, the thought of going on a bus tour with fifty people I had never met would have filled me with horror. Who wants to be herded around like cattle? How can anybody stand to be told what to do every morning?

This summer, however, the thought of seeing eight ball games in eight different parks with no worries over hotels, parking, tickets, or city driving was irresistible.

The tour starts with Wrigley Field in Chicago, a sacred destination for most baseball fans. From there we go to Cincinnati, Baltimore, Yankee Stadium in New York, Fenway

Park in Boston, the Hall of Fame in Cooperstown, NY, Cleveland, Detroit, and back to Chicago for a game at the ballpark formerly known as Comiskey.

The main attraction for me is Fenway Park in Boston. Built in 1912, Fenway is a crammed onto a single city block. It has no parking. Home runs bounce onto the street. The park has never been remodeled and is structurally unsound. It may be condemned at any time.

But at Fenway, according to one person I spoke to last week, "you can hear the voices." Ted Williams. Johnny Pesky. Carl Yastremski. Carlton Fisk.

Fenway is where a young left-handed pitcher named Babe Ruth pitched the Red Sox to a World Series win in 1918. Two years later, the Red Sox sold the Babe to the Yankees for $125,000. The Red Sox owner used the money to finance a musical called "No No Nanette," which failed.

The Yankees quickly discovered that Ruth could hit even better than he could pitch. They sent the Babe to right field and put up Yankee Stadium, "The House that Ruth Built," to hold the crowds who came to watch.

Meanwhile in Boston, the Ruth trade brought a hex down upon Fenway Park. The Red Sox have never won a World Series since Ruth pitched them to a title in 1918. In the same time, the Yankees have won the Series twenty-six times.

The Fenway Faithful, as Red Sox fans are called, are even more accustomed to heartache than Cubs fans. The Cubs, after all, won the Series as recently as 1945. But the rest of the time, the Cubs have stunk. Cubs fans are used to losing.

The Red Sox, meanwhile, are always in the hunt to the end, tantalizing their long-suffering fans with great teams and wonderful players who just can't win the big one.

So, I look forward to Fenway, to hearing the voices, to seeing the mound where Babe Ruth threw, and to hear the bitterest fans in the game hurl insults at the opposition.

Wrigley Field

In last week's column, I incorrectly stated that the Cubs last won the World Series in 1945. I regret the error. They won the National League pennant in 1945, but lost the Series. In fact, the Cubs last won a Series in 1908, a full decade before the Boston Red Sox won their last title.

This stuff matters at old Wrigley Field, the first stop on our tour of major league ballparks. Wrigley reeks of history, and the Cubs fans in the stands are ready to turn around and set the record straight if you open your mouth without knowing what you're talking about.

Cubs fans are a strange lot. Losing doesn't affect their loyalty. They are as devoted to their ballpark and its history as they are to the team. In fact, the only fan club I spotted at the game consisted of twenty beer-gutted men wearing t-shirts honoring the Cubs' equipment manager, now in his sixtieth year of service.

Fans from around the nation flock to Wrigley for the ambiance. The ivy on the outfield wall. The rickety grandstands in the outfield. The old scoreboard. The tight dimensions. The rusty catwalks under the stands.

For our group, the ambiance included being seated so deep beneath the upper deck that any ball hit in the air disappeared immediately from our view. We were right behind home plate, but a steel pillar blocked my view of the batter's box.

We didn't complain. On this stagnant, sultry August afternoon, it was a relief to be in the shade. And in the bottom of the sixth, our bad seats proved to be a godsend.

Because I couldn't see the batter's box, I spent the game scanning the rest of the field and the stands with my binoculars. As the Cubs came to bat in the bottom of the sixth, I was focused on the center field bleachers.

I noticed a few of the bleacher bums start to wave their shirts. Others waved their Cubs hats. Soon, I could see women digging in their purses for Kleenex to wave, or programs. Those without anything else to wave waved their hands.

Another bizarre Wrigley tradition, I decided. They're just trying to get the Cubs going by doing some strange dance.

But the waving became more violent. People took off their shirts to wave them in the air. Others ran up and down the aisles. It finally became obvious that the right field stands were being attacked by a cloud of insects.

It was a plague of millions of gnats. It eventually spread to the lower fifty rows of the entire stadium, which exempted us. It looked as if most in the crowd of 40,000 had gone stark raving mad.

The first on the field to be attacked was the third base umpire. He waved his hat in front of his face, tried to run away, and had all he could do to collect himself before each pitch.

After he reached first, Kenny Lofton was attacked. He stole second anyway. Cub left fielder Moises Alou wasn't so lucky. After the Cub trainer pulled a dead gnat out of his eye, he took three straight strikes and slammed his bat into the ground.

The players in the dugouts put towels over their heads. Some fans took refuge from the gnats in the higher reaches of the stadium. But Cubs fans being Cubs fans, nobody left.

The fans stayed and fought the gnats as the Cubs blew a one-run lead in the ninth. They stayed after Enemy Team took the lead. They stayed until their hero Sammy Sosa grounded meekly to the pitcher to end the game.

Only then did anybody leave. And true to form, there was no gloom, no mention of the Cubs loss. No, it had been a great game. Two close plays at the plate. A double-steal attempt. Three home runs. A couple of arguments. Good pitching. Good defense. Good baseball.

As we fought our way to our bus out on Waveland Avenue, the throng of 40,000 flooded the bars and burger joints around the ballpark in a jubilant mood. The Cubs had lost again, but it was a beautiful Saturday in Chicago, and the night had just begun.

Fenway Park

As we moved from city to city on our tour of major league ballparks, the forty-four baseball fans on our bus compared notes and debated the merits of each stadium.

We agreed that Fenway Park in Boston, a mecca for baseball fans due to its quirky dimensions and 90 years of history, exceeded our expectations, as did Wrigley Field in Chicago. Beyond their obvious architectural charms, both parks were packed to capacity with knowledgeable and enthusiastic fans who stayed until the final out.

Yankee Stadium in the Bronx was the biggest disappointment. A bungled mid-1970s renovation robbed the "House that Ruth Built" of its history and character. Today, Yankee Stadium has all the charm of a high school gym. Many fans left long before the game ended.

Oriole Park at Camden Yards in Baltimore, the first of the well-designed new generation ballparks, was classy and dignified in every detail. Jacobs Field in Cleveland had the best food, the best sight-lines, plus a fireworks show after the game that knocked the crowd flat.

Most of us felt that the architects of the new Great American Ballpark in Cincinnati botched a golden opportunity. Although the Ohio River runs right behind the right field fence, the view of the river is blocked by a grandstand. In addition, the ballpark is done in such a bright red that you feel as if you are in the world's largest Target store.

Fenway Park in Boston topped them all, but for different

reasons than expected. We anticipated the ambiance of history, the cramped quarters, and the close-up views of the players. We did not anticipate the rabid intensity of the Red Sox fans.

Fenway holds 33,500. The night we attended, 35,070 fans packed the stands and the aisles. Face value for tickets near the dugouts was $275. Scalpers were selling them for much higher, and this was just a regular season game.

With their ace Pedro Martinez on the mound, the Red Sox fans hung on every pitch. Almost nobody left their seats during an inning. They chanted, cheered, groaned, booed, and jeered every move. Late in the game, they stood every time Pedro worked the count to two strikes.

When Boston center fielder Johnny Damon climbed the center field fence to pull down a long drive, the crowd roared for the next several pitches, until Damon finally tipped his cap. With screaming fans hanging from the rafters of the ancient park, the game felt like a World Series.

When Martinez emerged from the dugout to start the ninth inning, he was greeted with a hearty roar. But Pedro was tired. He walked a batter, and gave up a couple of ringing hits. With two out, the bases were loaded and the game hung in the balance.

The crowd stood and cheered Pedro on. The count went full. The batter fouled off pitch after pitch.

Finally, Pedro reached back and threw a hard fastball. The pitch floated high and outside, but the umpire, apparently thinking the game had gone on long enough, threw out his arm, called strike three, and sent the Fenway faithful into a wild frenzy.

I looked around at our group. Only one of us was a Red Sox fan, but everybody was smiling, laughing, exchanging high fives. All of us, from ages 15 to 82, had dreamed for years of seeing Fenway Park. But none of us expected to have that much fun.

Sheppard and Faust

Many of the highlights of seeing eight baseball games in eight different stadiums in nine days came from activity off the field.

It was a privilege to hear firsthand the booming baritone of Yankee Stadium's legendary public address announcer Bob Sheppard. Sheppard has been the voice of Yankee Stadium for over fifty years.

A longtime speech teacher and a stern professional, Sheppard introduces each player with equal care. He studies hard and pronounces every name perfectly, even if it means rolling the R's in Rafael Palmiero's name, something nobody else, including Palmiero himself, bothers to do.

A rookie fresh up from Columbus gets precisely the same professional treatment as Sheppard gave Mickey Mantle, Yogi Berra, or Reggie Jackson. If Babe Ruth himself were to come back from the grave and pinch hit for the Yankees with the bases loaded in the bottom of the ninth, Sheppard would remain completely unemotional, and would likely introduce the Bambino as "George Ruth."

Another legend is Chicago White Sox organist Nancy Faust. Regarded as the best in her trade, Faust specializes in obscure musical puns. She creates one for every player, home or away, and you can entertain yourself throughout the game by trying to figure them out.

Some are easy. For example, when the Oakland A's sent Billy McWilliams to the plate, Faust played a line from the 1970s hit "Billy, Don't Be A Hero." When an opposing player had to return to the batter's box after a long foul ball, Faust played the Beatles' "Get Back To Where You Once Belonged."

Other of Faust's puns are more difficult. The introduction of Oakland A's second baseman Mark Ellis brought a line from Jefferson Airplane's "White Rabbit." It took us a while to figure out that the song contains the phrase "Just ask Alice, when she's ten feet tall." Ellis, Alice, get it?

I was proud to decipher one particular pun: when an A's batter received a walk, Faust played a little ditty I remembered from high school band called "Baby Elephant Walk." Only true baseball nuts would know that for a few years in the 1910s, the A's wore a baby elephant emblem on their uniforms.

American League officials long ago banned Faust from playing "Three Blind Mice" after a questionable call by the umpires, but that doesn't prevent her from innocently choosing tunes by Stevie Wonder or Ray Charles when she thinks the White Sox got the wrong end of a decision.

I have been a fan of Faust since I used to listen to White Sox broadcasts late at night on WGN Chicago during the 1970s. Soon after we entered the stadium, I asked an usher to show me where she sits during games.

The old usher grabbed my arm and pulled me along while he told me stories about Faust. She is the longest-serving White Sox employee. She doesn't read notes. She's flown in by sports teams to play in stadiums all over the country.

Finally, the usher pushed open a door and told me to look in. There was Faust pounding out a tune. When she finished, I introduced myself. Upon hearing that I was from Minnesota, Faust turned back to her keyboard and played a spirited version of the University of Minnesota fight song.

Faust happily signed my ticket stub. I went away as thrilled as a kid who just got an autograph from Barry Bonds. Players come and go, after all, but long-serving public address announcers and organists can attain the status of historic landmarks.

Baseball Bus

In the scurry and bustle of the modern world, it isn't always easy to find or keep friends. People move. Jobs change. People seem to yearn for some common bond, some glue to hold them together, but such a glue is often difficult to find.

Community ties were strong during settlement and throughout the Depression. It was a struggle to survive, and people needed each other. As tough as those times were, many old-timers today seem nostalgic for the days when neighbors were neighbors.

War is hell, but those guys who flew or fought together in World War II formed lasting ties. They still get together, even as they advance into their eighties. They faced adversity together, and the bonds they formed were strong.

Disasters such as floods or windstorms do tremendous damage. At the same time, you hear often of people who form lasting friendships during the recovery with people they didn't know before. "We got to know them during the flood," they say of people who are now fast friends.

So, how do we form friendships with others without having to endure war, disaster or grinding poverty?

When I signed up for my recent bus trip to eight baseball stadiums, the thought of being on a bus for ten days with 44 people I had never met caused me some anxiety. What if some of them are obnoxious or don't show up on time? How long will it be until my nerves are totally frayed?

The people on the tour ranged in age from 15 to 82. They

came anywhere from Massachusetts to Minnesota to California. We had lawyers, accountants, teachers, a rock concert promoter, a retired professor, one former minor league ballplayer, a college student, and a car dealer.

Ten days is a long time to be with any group of people, but we shared a love for baseball. As we whiled away the long hours stuck in traffic in Chicago, New York and Boston, good humor prevailed. Baseball stories flew back and forth. Laughter was constant.

Sometimes the good-natured discussion would reach disagreement. What year did the Braves move from Boston to Milwaukee? Where did Luis Tiant start his career?

For answers, we yelled up to the front of the bus to Bob, our resident baseball trivia expert. When he didn't know, and that wasn't very often, we had Jim hook up his laptop computer to his cell phone, get on the Internet, and soon the disagreement would be resolved.

Each day, it seemed, somebody on the bus had a birthday, so we sang and had treats. As the self-appointed tour choral director, I forced the whole bus to learn the Twins' theme song, which we sang as loud as we could in the stands during the fifth inning of the game in Detroit.

A dignified elderly couple became grandparents to those of us on the back of the bus. Warren and Teresa were all class, with a twinkle in their eye, a warm greeting every morning, and never a complaint. I suspect that their stately presence helped bring out the best in the rest of us.

All of us had our quirks, but a general attitude of tolerance and good manners held sway. So, it was sad to get off the bus and part ways. None of us will forget the ten golden August days we spent traveling from ballpark to ballpark, talking baseball, cracking jokes, enjoying the camaraderie that comes from a shared love of the game.

We may never meet again, but for ten days at least, baseball turned out to be a pretty good glue.

CHAPTER THREE

ARIZONA

Tucson

Greetings from Tucson, Arizona, a city with a scruffy charm that never disappoints. This is my fourth trip here, and I am sure there will be many more.

Why do I like Tucson so much?

First, the sunshine. It never ends. Day after day of perfect weather. Every morning is as pristine as a clear May morning in Minnesota. At night the air is crisp, in the forties, and flavored with wisps of mesquite smoke.

The forecast for Tucson? Sunny and seventy tomorrow, sunny and sixty-five the next day, sunny and sixty-eight the next, the same thing the day after that–good night everyone, stay tuned for sports.

The mountains. Although the city itself is on a plain, Tucson is surrounded by mountains and cliffs. From all around the perimeter of the city, hiking trails lead deep into rocky canyons and into forests of mighty 200-year old saguaro cactus.

The elevation. Tucson is at 3,000 feet. At such elevations, the sky turns deeper blue, the cliffs glow deeper red, the tangerines on the trees become a brighter orange, and the distant mountains fade to a richer purple at sunset.

The food. Down here they have fresh Mexican food, not the microwaved stuff with rubber cheese melted on top that you get back home.

My favorite Mexican grill, La Salsa, has nine different salsas, each made fresh every morning. Mango, tomatillo, avocado, cilantro and carrot salsas–in addition to the typical tomato and onion ones. I am going to eat my way through their menu before I leave.

Funky people. There are real hobos here, riding around on their rattletrap bikes, their skin tanned to leather. I suppose they are the riff-raff we talk about up north, the people the cold keeps out. But I kind of like them.

Tucson draws interesting people of all sorts, from pencil-necked, mush-minded liberal environmentalists to right-wing, red-necked, AK-47 toting bigots; from retired New York mobsters to retired Fergus Falls farmers.

There are run-of-the-mill suburban type people, those who chase around in their minivans confident they'll eventually find happiness on sale at the mall for 25% off. But in Tucson, suburbanites seem like a minority.

And there are simply no neighborhoods in Tucson that look anything like a suburb. Even in wealthy neighborhoods the homes are stucco, low in profile, and often obscured by masses of cactus. Nothing like Edina.

There is pollution. There is crime. There are bad neighborhoods. There is litter, and there is a lot of traffic. Developers gulp up the desert at a frightening pace.

But none of that stuff seems to matter. In fact, every time I visit Tucson, it isn't long before I get sad knowing I will eventually have to leave.

Development

Arizona is doomed to development and population increase. It doesn't take many sunny eighty degree days in January for one to figure out why.

The local paper here in Tucson is filled with the problems of expansion. Zoning disputes. Overcrowded schools. Attempts to preserve the desert. Water problems.

Most people here aren't natives, but once they've moved here they seem to do all they can to shut the door behind them. Yes, they live in a new development, but they don't want another new development on the other side of the fence.

There is no shortage of hiking trails in and around Tucson, but there are very few ball fields for the kids. Grass doesn't grow naturally, and every time somebody tries to build a park, the retirees, who don't care about ball fields, raise concerns over water use, traffic, noise, crime, whatever they can come up with to put the ball field on hold.

Neighbors protest the new Home Depot, but it goes up anyway after assurances from the company that they will be a good neighbor and that the masses of customers they draw will drive nice and slow on local streets and try to avoid hitting dogs and children.

We civic-minded, far-sighted citizens of rural northwestern Minnesota have a thing or two to teach these Arizonans, that is for sure.

Most of our towns have had no trouble keeping Home Depot out. With few exceptions, Wal-mart has been kept at bay, and chain restaurants are prohibited except for those pizza counters at Cenex.

We have maintained large spaces of green grass in the form of football fields, softball fields, fairgrounds, parks, playgrounds, and endless yards. If enrollment continues to decline, our goal of one acre of mowed grass per child will be attained early in 2010.

We have maintained strict limits on our population, forcing the biggest polluters, people between the ages of eighteen and sixty, to move away and do their polluting in the suburbs.

We have managed our water supply so well that for the past few years we have had a surplus, which we are more than willing to sell to those willing to suck it out of our basements or off of our wheat fields.

Environmental consciousness runs high. Wheat prices have been kept so low that it no longer pays to clear trees to create new farmland. Thousands of farmers have selflessly put their land in CRP in order to provide enhanced habitat for the endangered pocket gopher.

The greatest stroke of genius, however, has been the maintenance of bone chilling cold for five months per year. Nothing we have done in rural Minnesota has done more to keep out large technology corporations, families with small children, factories, industry, diversity, and other evils.

Yes, it is lucky we in Minnesota don't have eighty degree weather in January or soon we'd be the ones stuck dealing with new Home Depots, Wal-marts, strip malls, supermarkets and six lane streets.

Those are my thoughts as I sit caught in Tucson traffic, windows down, in shorts and t-shirt, bopping my hand against the side of my pickup to the beat of the radio on the fifth of January.

Finger Rock Trail

On Tucson's local news one night a retired cardiologist suggested that, for the good of their hearts, senior citizens should take a hike up the Finger Rock trail in the Catalina mountains north of the city. He smirked at the end, but I didn't know why.

Finger Rock is a pillar-like formation near the top of the Catalina range. It looked to me like a pretty tame climb. If senior citizens could do it, I figured I should have no problem.

Just to be safe, I took a quart of water along, as well as two of those yucky health bars, and a notebook for recording profound thoughts.

About one-half hour up the trail I stopped to rest, proud of how far I had come. Ah, the wilderness! I heard some water gurgling and drifted off the trail to find the stream.

Thirty feet in I found myself at the edge of somebody's yard. The gurgling was the swimming pool cleaning itself. I wasn't even out of the suburbs yet.

Soon, however, the trail headed straight up. Switchbacks. Cliffs. Cactus. Loose rocks. Dust. I saw very few hikers. I must be far beyond the senior citizen zone, I thought.

Every couple of hundred feet I climbed, the plant life changed. The giant saguaro disappeared, and gnarled junipers took their place.

In a dry stream bed stood a huge cottonwood, a rarity in Arizona. It was full of yellow leaves–in January, no less. I sat on a rock, swigged some water, choked down a health bar, and pulled out my notebook.

"The golden leaves of the cottonwood remind me of fall in Minnesota," I wrote. Also: "The more water I drink, the lighter my pack gets." Profound thoughts indeed. I packed up and trudged onward.

Things got hairy in a hurry. I don't mind heights when I am walking on a level trail. But when the trail itself slopes off sideways towards the abyss and there are no tree roots to grab, no ledges to catch, nothing but air–then I get nervous.

I ended up in a crab position, sliding towards nothingness. It was like sliding down a roof. The crumbling rock ate at my palms like shingles would. I eventually stopped sliding, but then froze in place for fear I would start sliding again.

Now I knew why the cagey old doctor had a smirk on his face. He and everybody else in Tucson knew it was a joke when he suggested Finger Rock Trail for heart patients.

I clung to the rock, not knowing where to turn. Eventually I heard voices. Help had arrived!

A fit and tan elderly couple popped around the corner. They were in their eighties, wrapped in Spandex, well-preserved. I tried to act cool and relaxed, and said hi.

They said hi, but didn't stop. They politely stepped around me and went on past, almost at a jog, loudly discussing condo association politics.

The mountain goat seniors inspired me to get on the move again, but in the opposite direction. I headed back down the mountain, my heart thumping faster than is safe or healthy.

Mt. Lemmon Highway

The southern Arizona desert is a flat plain. Out of that plain rise several small mountain ranges. Each range appears as if it is an island in a vast sea. The largest of these ranges, the Santa Catalina mountains, forms a twenty mile wall which towers over Tucson.

The Catalinas loom as high over Tucson as the Rocky Mountains rise above Denver. Yet to the untrained eye, the Catalinas look like little more than a pile of rocks one could climb in a spare afternoon.

It is an optical illusion. Unlike the Rockies, the Catalinas must be inspected up close to get a proper feel for their size. Hike a trail into the mountains and soon you are snaking through impressive canyons walled by massive cliffs. From the city, those cliffs look as if they are about thirty feet tall. Up close, it is obvious they measure 500 feet or more.

You quickly realize it would take far more than a spare afternoon to reach the top of the Catalinas on foot. Fortunately, one can drive to the top of the range on the Mt. Lemmon Highway.

The highway climbs more than 6,000 feet in thirty miles. The road is so curvy the trip takes over an hour. In those thirty miles, the temperature dips thirty degrees. You pass through five distinct climates before reaching the top.

The road starts in desert dominated by forests of the mighty saguaro cactus. A few miles up the saguaro disappear, replaced by oak and savannah grasslands. Some twists and turns later, the manzanita, a bizarre green shrub with a trunk the color of copper tubing, takes over.

All along, breathtaking vistas pop into view. The hairpin turns of the narrow road demand complete attention, so I pulled over to the side to gawk lest I end up in a ravine.

Eventually the manzanita give way to junipers, and finally the road tunnels through towering pine forests interspersed with groves of aspen, just like in Montana.

Less than an hour before, I had driven past a bank thermometer which read 80 degrees. Now, a wet blanket of snow lay on the floor of the pine forest.

Near the top, three minivans with plates from Mexico sat with doors wide open as about a dozen children tossed snowballs at each other, perhaps for the first time in their lives. A snowman from previous visitors stood off to the side, complete with a carrot nose.

By this time, it was three o'clock. My Norwegian blood was demanding coffee. I had been dreaming that there might be a nice little coffee shop at the top and sure enough, I was in luck.

An organic gourmet coffee shop, no less, with coffee made from beans harvested by virtuous Central American peasants clothed in natural fibers, and then roasted in kilns heated by domestic renewable fuels produced by vegetarian union labor.

And pecan pie! I told the kid to warm me up a slice. That'll be $5.81, he said, and I jumped back about a foot. Turns out the pie cost $4.75, and was not plain pecan pie, but "Chocolate Bourbon Pecan Pie." I said what the heck.

Despite its virtue, the coffee was lukewarm. But the pie was worth every cent, and I ate each bite very slowly, especially the layer of dark chocolate pudding. So much for virtue.

Once finished, I sat back. Sunshine filtered through the pines and filled the little mountain-top coffee shop with color. Thirty miles of coasting downhill lay ahead. It was pretty clear that climbing the Catalinas in a pickup was not a bad way to spend a spare afternoon.

Lazy Oldsters

I ain't prejudice or nothin, don't get me wrong, but if there's one thing about being in Arizona that's a little hard to take, it is all these lazy old white people shuffling around living off of government checks.

Trailer park after trailer park full of people who did all their business somewhere else and moved here just to sit around.

You can't get them to do no work. No sir. It's always this or that, grandkids, golf, flea markets, card games, always something.

And it's not that they're stupid. Not at all. I talked to a local mechanic, and he said when it comes to cars and things, they know their stuff.

He told me about old white men who hang around his shop and shoot the bull and then they point out just exactly what's wrong with the car, and they're usually right. But try to hand them a wrench and they high-tail it back to Buena Vista trailer park faster than you can say Judge Judy.

Some will work a little bit, but they won't take no money for it. See, if they take any money then they don't get their government check. Sort of makes you sick, doesn't it, the way this country operates?

Then, because they don't take no money, they feel they can show up when they want to and not show up when they don't want to and it just gets to be more hassle than it's worth, not knowing who's going to be where when. It's too bad, but it ain't worth hiring them, even the good ones.

Then when one of them trips over the flag stick on the 5th green and breaks a hip, who pays for that? The taxpayer. Yes sir, through Medicare and Medicaid, or the county.

The worst of it is, if the county doesn't pick up their whole tab they practically have a stroke—and the government has to pay for that too. It just goes on.

"We paid in," they say, as if they are entitled to all this. Yeah right. All the money they put in long ago went to buy screwdrivers and toilet seats for the Pentagon. Don't kid with me.

No, it's my hard earned money that they're getting. I'll bet it isn't one week after they take the money out of my check that it ends up in a slot machine somewhere, or in the pocket of some hip surgeon.

Good thing there's the Latinos down here to pay taxes and keep the economy going. They work hard and don't complain. They run the restaurants, pull the teeth, fix the hips, pave the roads, and restock the shelves at Wal-Mart.

No sir, if it weren't for the hard-working Latinos, this place would just be one big welfare colony.

Patagonia

For a Sunday afternoon drive, I took a two-lane road south of Tucson and ended up in a little town a dozen miles north of the Mexican border called Patagonia.

Perhaps because it is as crumbling and decrepit as any dying small town in the Midwest, Patagonia charmed me right away. Boarded up store fronts. Porches sagging with junk. Empty lots grown up in weeds and crammed with rusting cars.

But the school looked new, and was flanked by irrigated ballfields. Mass had just finished at the little Catholic church, and huge Latino families poured out onto the dried-brown grass in their Sunday best. Tattered cowboy hats sauntered out of the little Ma and Pa cafe after a leisurely Sunday breakfast.

Patagonia is snuggled in a picturesque valley between two dignified desert mountain ranges. Through town runs a river which has created what is called a "riparian" forest, a grouping of trees which forms in the desert due to an almost continual presence of water.

And so Patagonia is shaded by an oasis of cottonwood, walnut, and old gnarled live oak, a type of oak which doesn't lose its leaves. Because such a grouping of trees is so rare in the desert southwest, birds flock to Patagonia–two-hundred and seventy-five species of birds, according to a pamphlet from the Nature Conservancy.

Patagonia is at 5,000 feet elevation. Its summers are cool. Its air is clean and crisp. The evenings call for a crackling fire every night of the year, according to a pamphlet from the Chamber of Commerce.

Scenery, birds, peace and quiet only an hour from bustling

Tucson: clearly, Patagonia is doomed. There are early signs, which I didn't notice until my second slow cruise around town—discreet little signs in fancy calligraphy.

Licensed acupuncturist. Medicinal herb consultant. Yoga instructor. Art gallery. On the edge of town outside the gates of an enormous estate was the kicker, a classy sign which said: "Life Rejuvenation Centre."

One can only assume that a Life Rejuvenation Centre is where, for $2500 per week, you can bask in the desert sunshine, get your face caked in mud, have a pedicure, get a massage and consult with a professional spiritual advisor, all at the same time.

Poor Patagonia. It has been discovered by the SUV bunch. Soon it will be overwhelmed by frazzled wealthy coastal types who see in its peace, quiet, calm and quaintness a possible cure for their many psychological problems.

Money will be no object. Old buildings will be turned into boutiques. Dumpy houses on Main Street will sprout neon signs and smell of gourmet coffee. Property values will skyrocket. The locals will wonder what hit them.

The newcomers will bring their stress with them. There will be zoning disputes. The new Italian restaurant and a sparkling convenience store will combine to kill off the Ma and Pa cafe. The Broken Wheel will close when Bill and Marie decide it just makes too much sense to sell their liquor license to the new sports bar.

I felt like an intruder tiptoeing around with my Minnesota plates. I could see suspicion in the eyes of the locals as I drove past the church, the cafe, the bustling little grocery mart. They like that you like their town, but they hate what you might do to it.

I could offer to cure their problem. My advice would be simple: the Patagonians should just turn down the thermostat about one hundred degrees, level those darn mountains and saw down those pesky trees in the river bottom. Then their charming village could forever remain as pure as any Midwestern farm town.

Seeing Stars

Tucson's clear desert skies make it a haven for astronomers. City ordinances control outdoor lighting so city lights don't obscure the stars. Back yard observatories number in the hundreds. The largest collection of telescopes in the world is perched on Kitt Peak, forty miles to the west.

I have always wanted to look through a powerful telescope. I heard that a Tucson astronomy club has a spot in the desert where they gather twice a month on moonless nights. I looked on the internet and found directions to the spot. I also found out they planned to meet there last night.

The spot was remote. Twenty miles outside the city limits the road turned to gravel and went over two rumbling one-lane bridges before running through a ranch yard and into a pitch dark desert clearing.

A kid who looked about twelve ran towards my pickup with a dim red flashlight, opened the passenger door and said, "Could you use just your parking lights, please?" Oops. I had already managed to offend the people I had hoped were going to let me see the stars.

Not to worry. I parked, and as soon as I shut the door of my pickup, the kid said, "Wanna see Saturn?"

Of course. I looked in the eyepiece of his telescope, which was nearly as tall as he. There was Saturn, just as in the pictures, the rings casting a deep shadow on the golden globe of planet itself.

The kid, who introduced himself as Nick, took me to the

next telescope where his father was delivering an impromptu lecture to three Australians who kept interrupting him with questions about UFOs. It was so dark I could see none of their faces.

The Australians eventually got cold and left, and I was treated to a private tour of the sky from a man who turned out to be one of the professionals at the Kitt Peak observatory. Almost as impressive as his knowledge of the sky was his ability to explain the stars in terms I could easily understand.

He had a method of pointing out even the tiniest stars in the sky, and soon I had spotted the only space object visible to the naked eye outside of our galaxy—the Andromeda galaxy, one and a half-million light years away, so dim that you have to avert your eyes from it just a little to make it appear at all.

Through the telescope we looked at the Orion nebula, an astoundingly colorful cloud of gas which has produced dozens of new stars, a cluster of which sparkled within the multi-colored cloud like a handful of diamonds in a velvet-lined box.

Nick hollered from his telescope that he had found a new galaxy. New to him at least. He ran over to their minivan with his red flashlight to enter the find in his logbook.

It was only then I realized that there were dozens of little observing parties around the clearing. Each telescope was identifiable only by the dim red lights blinking at the base of its tripod. I walked from station to station. Each telescope focused on something different.

I saw Jupiter and four of its moons. I saw a star cluster so dense that stars packed the tiny stretch of sky visible in the eyepiece like sparkling grains of sand on the beach. I saw that the North Star, when magnified, is actually a pair of stars.

As I pulled back onto the dirt road, my head was swimming. I was so distracted by what I had seen that it took me a minute or two to realize that the radio was quietly playing the song "Knock, Knock, Knockin on Heaven's Door."

Leaving Tucson

A rare two days of clouds and rain made leaving Tucson slightly less difficult, but only slightly. For ease of access, I threw my winter jacket over the top of the boxes underneath the tarp in the pickup box, but didn't really believe I would need to wear it two days later.

I remember my first trip to Arizona in the winter of 1995. When I stepped off the train onto the platform in Tucson, I felt hot sun on my face in January for the first time in my life. My mood lifted. I had energy. I didn't want to leave.

I have been back five times, and the effects have never dulled. I have found Arizona in winter to be a powerful mood-altering substance, available without a doctor's prescription.

Minnesota's cold winters drag me down and always have. In the elementary grades, I invariably spent most of February home with lingering diseases of one sort or another. My first grade class sent me a card saying that the gerbils missed me.

That pattern continued through college when I found it very difficult to drag myself from bed to attend class in January and February. When I made it to lectures, I nodded off or sat there in a numb daze. What a mistake to take Ancient Roman history in the winter! A surer cure for insomnia has yet to be devised.

After college, it just got worse. I could work long hours and have fun in spring, summer and fall, but when I tried to work in winter, I couldn't cut it. Over the years, I quit school twice and left several jobs in either February or March.

So, when I felt the effects of the Arizona sunshine for the first time, I resolved to sneak away and bask in the warmth as many winters as possible—and right away, not after my joints have rusted in place and my interests have narrowed to whist.

Not a lot goes on back here in the middle of winter anyway, at least for those of us in seasonal work. People start living for high school ball games. Or they linger at the cafe from breakfast until noon. Or they watch so much television news that they turn into nervous wrecks.

Some people ice fish or drive snowmobile, but those activities freeze my extremities. Plus, I would be the one to fall through the hole in the ice or run into an oak tree with the snowmobile, probably on the same day.

My Arizona life is almost monastic. This trip I stayed in a little apartment furnished with an air mattress, two folding tables, two folding chairs, an old stuffed chair I eventually left in the dumpster, and a box of books.

But the luxury of walking outside without a jacket! Of hiking in the mountains, of watching the dazzling Arizona sunsets! Of driving with your window down at 9 p.m. in January! Of real Mexican food!

Of course it had to end sometime. Reality hit when I had to dig my jacket out of the pickup box in York, Nebraska. I was driving in thick fog, and it was getting colder.

My windshield wipers iced up twenty miles later. Sleet turned to snow at the Nebraska-South Dakota border. By Sioux Falls, winds reached 45 mph, and visibility was down to almost nothing. The temperature had plummeted forty degrees in three hours of driving.

A few hours later, my pickup's tires crunched over the snow in my driveway. It took 4-wheel drive to get through the big drift in front of the garage. The cold air crinkled my nostrils. Cacti and burritos were but a distant memory.

Goodbye Summerhaven

Last winter, I climbed the Mt. Lemmon highway with my pickup and reached Summerhaven, Arizona, a tiny resort town near the top of the mountain shaded by hundred-foot high pine, most of them hundreds of years old.

Mt. Lemmon overlooks Tucson. A winding, hour-long drive from the desert below, Summerhaven is a favorite haunt for Tucsonians eager to escape the summer heat.

It was eighty degrees on the desert floor last January when I started the climb out of Tucson. Thirty miles of highway later, I watched children throw snowballs in the shade of the pine near the ski resort at the top of Mt. Lemmon.

I don't go to Arizona to see snow, but it was fun to watch the children spill out of minivans with Mexican plates to frolic in a substance they had never seen before. Snow can be fun stuff, I was reminded, if you aren't buried in it five months per year.

Once I reached Summerhaven, I found a little coffee shop where I enjoyed a slice of supremely decadent chocolate-pecan pie. As I watched the high-altitude sunlight, filtered by the pine needles, stream onto the wood floor of the bright little shop, I thought I had found a slice of heaven.

Last week, a fire swept through Summerhaven, destroying the pine trees, as well as over two hundred homes.

I held out hope that the coffee shop, snuggled as it was in a little hollow with a few other stores and homes, somehow escaped the fire.

But while searching the internet, I ran across a story in the *New York Times* which contained an interview with the coffee shop's owner. His shop and all the buildings in that little hollow had been destroyed.

There must be great sadness in Tucson, and not just for the people who lost homes. Summerhaven was a treasure. If you asked natives to suggest places to visit, a trip up the Mt. Lemmon highway was at the top of their list.

A friendly Latino gentleman behind the counter at a Mexican restaurant wanted to make sure I had been up to Mt. Lemmon. He goes there with friends on weekends, he said. They park down the mountain a ways, hike up some cliffs, have pie at the coffee shop, and hike back down to their cars.

Burned buildings can be a tragedy, but usually only for those who lived or did business in them. Buildings can be rebuilt. However, the towering pine which surrounded Summerhaven will not be replaced for generations.

I take comfort in revisiting favorite places and seeing that they are the same. Last summer, I revisited the monstrous cathedral in the tiny town of Ely, England. It was even more enchanting than I had remembered from my visit fifteen years before.

Other landmarks on my list: Douglas Lodge at Itasca. The lift bridge in Duluth. The state capitol building in St. Paul. The truck stop in Clearwater, MN, where you can buy the best blueberry fritter bread in the world.

I rely upon such places to never change. In fact, revisiting such landmarks gets better as you get older–in part, because you change and they don't.

Sadly, residents of Tucson will have to strike Summerhaven from their list of valued landmarks. So will visitors from all over the world, including myself, who found the place enchanted and planned to return.

CHAPTER FOUR

EUROPE

London

If I make it out of England without getting flattened by a speeding car, I will be lucky. They drive on the left side of the road here, and I am perpetually looking the wrong way before I cross the street.

You can't undo a lifetime of habit in one week. I look both ways several times, then sprint across. I doubt I will ever be able to predict what is going to happen at English intersections, so I cross only in the middle of the block.

The streets are narrow, and some of the sidewalks are less than three feet wide. Despite the tight quarters, cars speed along at 30-40 miles-per-hour. Step off the curb to let a lady with bags of groceries past, and you might get plowed over by a speeding Renault.

To get some practice crossing streets and to ease my nerves, I picked the tiny town of Rye in southeastern England out of the guidebook, and went there for a day.

To reach Rye, I had to transfer trains several times out of London. Each train was smaller and more rickety than the last. That was reassuring. I was sure I was going somewhere sleepy and remote.

But as the old train lurched into the station at Rye, I saw dozens of tour buses and hundreds of cars parked in a field near the station. The lovely little town was overrun by British tourists.

Crossing the street was more hazardous in Rye than in London. The streets of Rye were last widened in the mid-

1300s, and consisted of one lane of cobblestone. The side-walks were at times less than two feet across.

Finally, I learned to just tag along with a local. When they crossed, I crossed. If they waited, I waited–even if there isn't a car in sight.

The confusion over crossing the street goes both ways. When the British travel abroad, they report the same problem in reverse.

In fact, if I get hit by a car, I will be in good company: while visiting New York City in the mid-1930s, Winston Churchill stepped off the curb on 5th Avenue, looked the wrong way, and was flattened by a taxi.

Churchill nearly died. He spent months in the hospital. He suffered pain from the accident for the rest of his life.

Fortunately, Churchill recovered well enough to lead England and the Allies to victory over Hitler in World War II. If that taxi had been going any faster, England might still be under German control.

Yes, it is difficult to overestimate the importance of looking both ways before crossing the street.

Paris

The French drive on the right side of the road, but that doesn't make crossing the street here any easier than it was in London.

Street lights in Paris are just for decoration. They turn green, red and yellow, but the French cross at their own whim, according to rules I have not yet figured out.

I tried my method of attaching myself to a local and crossing with them. It did not work. I followed a young man as he scooted between the parked cars and out into the street. He bolted into traffic, and I followed.

I lost my nerve when he bounced off a speeding Audi as if it were a would be tackler. He made it across, and I hope he gets his Heisman trophy, but I was left behind, stuck between two lanes of traffic going *schoom schoom schoom* inches past me on either side.

Finally, traffic jammed up ahead enough for me to make a dash for the sidewalk. So much for that method.

Now, I latch on to decrepit elderly folks and cross only when they cross. They provide good cover, although they aren't always handy when you need them.

The ultimate nightmare intersection in Paris, and perhaps the world, is at the Arc de Triomph, where twelve streets meet in a big circle. Cars enter the circle, which is eight lanes wide, drive around for a while, and spin off when they find the street they want.

I watched for ten minutes, but I couldn't figure out the

rules to this intersection, either. They didn't even bother to put up traffic lights at the Arc, but they did provide underground tunnels for pedestrians, for which I was thankful.

People know that you are American in Paris. I don't know what it is. They wear jeans and tennis shoes, too, so that isn't it. Americans must just carry themselves differently.

As I was returning to my hotel last night, I scurried across a particularly harrowing intersection. I made it across, scooted through the six inch space between two parked cars, and jumped up on the curb where I paused to catch my breath.

While I was pulling myself together after the latest street crossing ordeal, a woman took my hand in a very kind manner and said, "You American, right?" I said yes, grateful for this smidgen of kindness in a bustling foreign capital.

"Would you like live show?" she said, and gestured grandly towards a theater-like storefront with curtains across the door.

At the risk of being rude, I apologized, told her I really had to get back to my hotel, and got the heck out of there.

All of this makes me wonder anew why in the world that chicken ever decided to cross the road.

Notre Dame

A highlight of my trip to Europe was visiting the Cathedral of Notre Dame in Paris and hearing its legendary pipe organ roar.

Europe's cathedrals are astounding. Most are longer than a football field and taller than a grain elevator. The steeple of the cathedral in Salisbury, England rises 404 feet. It was topped off in the 1300s.

Notre Dame is neither the largest cathedral in France, nor the most ornate. But while other cathedrals have become little more than tourist attractions, Notre Dame still plays a large role in the national life of France. Thousands turn out for masses on Sunday and throughout the week.

But I was most interested in the music. I had been warned by a friend back home that the Notre Dame pipe organ sounded, as he put it, "like a Versatile tractor bearing down on you at full throttle." Sounded good to me.

Late Sunday afternoon I ducked inside and found a seat. There was a concert in progress. The organ played softly, more like leaves rustling in a breeze than a tractor. It went on at that rate for twenty minutes–rain drops, birds chirping, and other such little sounds.

Then, the organist pulled out more and more stops. The breeze through the leaves turned into a gust. From off to the left came a bass note which sounded like a souped-up pickup rapping its pipes. A few seconds later, from the right, came the sound of a Mack truck shifting down on a steep hill.

As the piece neared its crescendo, the Versatile tractors joined in. At least three. At the same time, a thunderstorm gathered over the front altar and a fleet of F-16 fighter jets buzzed the sanctuary. Smoke billowed out and sparks flew from the pipes high overhead.

That is what it sounded like to me, anyway. The sounds from the organ were everything I had anticipated for all these years, and more.

After the concert, I toured the church. The stained glass was breathtaking, including a circular rose window at least sixty feet in diameter. I stared up at it until my neck was sore.

Suddenly, the organ fired up again, as violently as before. Evening mass was about to begin. A team of priests marched in processional to the altar, staffs in hand. The cathedral was jammed.

A battle began between the priests, who had their business to attend to, and the egotistical Notre Dame organist, who used every break in the liturgy to let loose another angry avalanche of sound which I suspect lasted far longer than the priests desired.

Meanwhile, the crowd of well over a thousand people milled about, as the French are prone to do, as if nothing was going on up front. A heavy aroma of incense, perfume, sweat and alcohol hung in the cavernous room.

As the sun set, the grand scene was lit by hundreds of candles. I snuck around the side and got as close to the altar as I could. The singing and liturgy were in French, of course, which only made it more mysterious. Billows of incense smoke mushroomed slowly through the fading shafts of sunlight to the ceiling eighty feet above.

Just then, I remembered: it was on this very altar where 200 years ago Napoleon was to be crowned Emperor by the Pope. At the last moment, in a move admired by Frenchmen to this day, the audacious leader snatched the crown from the Pope and put it on his own head.

As I watched the colorful and dramatic tableau at Notre Dame that Sunday night, that famous scene from the history books didn't seem so very far away.

Switzerland

Just inside the Swiss border, the difference between Switzerland and France became obvious. Suddenly, no litter, no dust, no grime.

A woman inadvertently dropped a plastic wrapper on the street in front of the Basel train station. It stayed on the ground less than five minutes before it was snatched up by a uniformed cleaner.

As I browsed the news stand while waiting for the next train, a man roared by on a sweeper. He dabbed at my feet with a broom, pulling invisible debris into the path of his sweeper machine.

The bathrooms at the train station were spotless. It cost $1.50 to use them, but oh well. Switzerland isn't the richest country in the world for nothing.

I returned to my hotel one day to find a pair of maids scrubbing the stairwell, the walls, the staircase, even the light switches. I am sure it was the second time that week, for the place shone before they started.

Swiss fastidiousness extends from the gardens, which remain lush and prim even in early September, to the masses of geraniums which hang from nearly every man-made precipice.

And then there are the peaks and natural precipices which tower over all of Switzerland, the grand Swiss Alps. I had somehow imagined that since the Alps have been traversed by man for centuries that they would look worn and tame.

They aren't tame. At their heights, the Alps are raw, sheer, dangerous and sharp, more ominous than the Rockies. Lower down, where the cliffs finally swoop outwards enough for grass to grow, intense cultivation begins.

Every strip of grass is valued in Switzerland. The rich green pasture land extends to places where walking takes you up more than over. The valleys are dark green, dotted with patches of forest. At the bottom of every one is a little village, each punctuated by a single church steeple.

Lucerne has many church steeples, but the two on the Holtkierke, the largest church in town, drew me inside. Given the rough stone exterior, I did not expect the interior of the 1634 church to be so polished.

It glowed. I couldn't find a speck of dust, and I looked for over an hour. The slate in the floor was polished, with no dust between the cracks. The ornately carved pews–hundreds of them–shone, not a dull or worn spot anywhere, even in the deepest crevasses. The stone pillars were whitewashed.

The many altars–each fifteen feet tall, impossibly ornate, covered in gold leaf–shone in the sun. No dust there. I rubbed my finger inside the base of a pew. Nothing. When the sun hit the silver chandeliers, they shone so that they were painful to view. Who does all this polishing?

I don't know what is most impressive about Switzerland, the famous alpine scenery, or the polish and neatness of the homes, yards and historic buildings. The country is pristine, from the largest of its mountains down to the light switches in the hotel lobby.

Italy

Cross the border from Switzerland into Italy and the sun begins to shine. Laundry hangs next to red geraniums from the balconies. Palms wave in the breeze. Grandmas fling open their shutters, plant their palms on the window sill, and preside over the busy street below.

The cheerful Italians contrast sharply with the sullen English, the surly French, and the robotically efficient Swiss. Italians are approachable. They greet you. If they don't know English, they launch into the universal language of charades.

The Italians come by charades naturally. Their hands wave as they talk—and they talk all of the time, it seems. Some stereotypes are rooted in truth.

I rode a morning commuter train into Venice. When the train stopped at a station, silencing the squeaking and rumbling, the train car was as loud with gabbing as a Lutheran church basement after a big funeral.

When I rode a morning commuter train from Cambridge into London, Englishmen jammed in the rail car were—well, more sullenly quiet than a Lutheran church at the mention of the term "fund drive."

I stayed with friends in Aviano, a small town in northeastern Italy close to the Yugoslav border, in the shadow of the impressive Dolomite mountains.

Wednesday is market day in Aviano, which means that dozens of carts pull into town loaded with vegetables, cheeses and fresh flowers. Other carts have cookware, toys, gifts—one was devoted solely to socks.

The whole town comes out, including dozens of grandmas on bicycles. Peddlers barter cheerfully with the customers. Everybody seems to have a good time, even those weighing out smelly fresh fish.

It is over by noon. By then, the sun is oppressively hot. Stores and banks close daily at a little past twelve, and reopen in late afternoon. You can't even get an ice cream cone–or the superior Italian equivalent, gelati–at two in the afternoon.

But if you need help, you'll find it. I asked directions on the train, and the conductor unleashed a torrent of Italian which I took to mean that I should get off at some town starting with an M.

I lied, said I understood, and waited for a town starting with M. When one arrived, the Italian woman across from me, who spoke no English, and who hadn't looked at me before, grabbed my arm.

She had understood the conductor, of course, and knew that I had not.

With a firm hand, she not only pulled me off the train, but tugged me over to the right platform for my connection, and gestured for me to stay planted right there. She then ran off to catch another train.

Such small gestures of kindness can shape one's view of an entire country, I find. When lost and confused in a foreign land, a helping hand from a stranger is no less than a gift from above.

Fast Train

In France, they have a handful of trains between major cities which travel as fast as 180 miles-per-hour.

High-speed trains sound like fun, but they're not. Things go by so fast at that speed that it makes you sick. To avoid nausea, nobody looks out the window. You either look straight ahead or read a book.

I tried to nap, but the on-off flashes of sunlight alternating with the darkness of tunnels and ravines penetrated my eyelids and prevented rest. It was torture.

The trip is done in a flash, and thank goodness. The high speed removes all fun from the journey, so it is just as well that the trip ends quickly.

The day before I boarded the high-speed train, I took a long walk in a forest on a plateau overlooking Lucerne, Switzerland. The trails were wide and well-traveled. There were signs giving directions to local villages. It was plain that these walking trails were used for more than recreational hikes.

Walking was the main mode of transport in Europe years ago. Martin Luther once walked from Germany to Rome. Bach toured Germany on foot, giving organ concerts wherever he found a church.

On those trails above Lucerne, I thought about the excitement of taking a long walking journey centuries ago. Can you imagine the people you'd meet in just one day with nobody cooped up in their fast-moving cars?

A business trip from Switzerland to Paris would take weeks on foot, but so what. You would see every detail between here and there, talk to the locals at every stop, hear the birds, the gurgling streams, watch the animals, see the views.

You would learn as much on the journey as you would at the destination. You would get exercise. With no electronic communication, problems at home couldn't send their tentacles through the phone lines to entangle you from afar.

And yet, because you were on business, you could deduct the whole experience, knowing that you had no choice but to travel as slow as molasses.

Winston Churchill lamented the speed of modern life. He observed that no invention had done more to make the world ugly than the internal combustion gas engine.

Churchill preferred horses. He wasn't big on trains, and, although he often went up front to take the controls of the planes he rode, he would have been just as happy if air travel had never been invented.

Churchill has a point. Gas engines make noise, cause smog, go too fast, encourage the building of enormous roads, and, as it turns out, have an unquenchable thirst for liquids found buried in regions of the world best left alone.

All of that trouble for speed. But just where does all of this speed get us? Whenever I enter the suburbs of Minneapolis after months of driving in the country, I am astounded by the breakneck pace of traffic, even on a Sunday afternoon.

The suburbanites look grimly determined to get where they are going. So determined, in fact, that if you get in their way and don't drive fast enough, I've heard that they'll shoot you.

To avoid meeting that fate, I try to keep up. But what I really want to do is ask them where they are going and why they have to get there so fast. If we were on foot, I could do that. But in my pickup, I can only grip the wheel, look straight ahead, and hope not to get shot.

There are advantages to high speed travel and communication. Poor Bach returned from one of his long journeys to find that his young wife had taken ill and died several weeks before. It took him years to recover from the tragedy.

Speed might be helpful in such an emergency, but most of the speed at which life moves today is unnecessary. Speedy transportation takes the joy out of the journey, and speedy communication keeps us in constant touch with people whose company we might enjoy more after an occasional long hiatus.

We can't go back, I suppose, but maybe we could learn to take it a little slow every now and then. We might find that no hurry means less worry.

Greenland

Midway through the flight from London to Minneapolis, the pilot announced that we were going to be treated to a clear view of Greenland, the world's largest island.

What a sight. I put down my book halfheartedly at the pilot's announcement, but when I spotted the first icebergs off Greenland's east coast, I sat forward in my seat and pressed my face against the airplane window like a kindergartner on a school bus.

From 30,000 feet, the view of the earth's surface is usually obscured by haze and clouds. But the air over Greenland this afternoon was crystal clear. Icebergs by the hundred glowed white in the deep blue waters of the north Atlantic.

The icebergs floated out from Greenland's fjords. On each side of the fjords rose rust-brown snow-capped mountains. As we moved inland at 600-miles-per hour, the fjords turned into broad rivers. Finally, each river abruptly ended with the sheer face of a glacier.

The glaciers, massive rivers of ice striped with gravel and rock, widened as our plane continued inland. They eventually disappeared, along with the mountains, underneath an endless field of perfect white.

That field of white is Greenland's massive ice cap, a monolith which contains enough water to raise the world's oceans 22 feet if it all were to melt. The ice cap alone covers sixteen times the area of England, and is up to two miles thick.

From our vantage point, the ice cap was as flat as the Red

River Valley–with one exception: a tip of a mountain poked through which created a snowdrift downwind which I figure was about five miles long.

We crossed only the southern tip of Greenland, so it wasn't long before we reached the opposite side of the ice cap. The gravel-striped glaciers reappeared, this time running west. They ended with tourquoise-colored rivers and iceberg-filled fjords. The rusty mountains came back into view.

At the base of the mountains on the coast was a faint fringe of green, the only green in the otherwise white and brown Greenland. On that fringe was a meager sign of human habitation, an air strip amidst a handful of farm houses.

Greenland's coast quickly disappeared behind us. Cloud cover once again obscured the Atlantic. Yet, it was a long time after our half hour trip across the island before I could settle back into my book.

I was beat from spending the previous few days in Paris and London. Paris, for all its charms, is dirty, smelly and crowded. And to describe the demeanor of the Parisien French in printable terms would be dishonest.

London is not much better. A day walking the streets of London leaves your throat raw from diesel fumes. And the only happy people in all of England seem to be the elderly and the children.

Seeing the crystal clear air and empty Arctic spaces of Greenland invigorated me, even from inside a stuffy plane. It made me want to travel there and find out what kind of people live in the little houses around the air strip, overlooking the massive icebergs in the harbor.

Travel Abroad

In May of 1988, I traveled to New Zealand for my student teaching assignment. I was to stay in the homes of other teachers in order to get a feel for New Zealand culture.

After the thirty hour flight, I was dropped off by a taxi at the modest home of a middle-aged couple in suburban Wellington. The husband was a government bureaucrat, and the wife was a teacher at the school where I was to teach.

An hour after I arrived at the home of my hosts, I caught sight of a note beside the fridge: "Pat, we can't find anybody else to host the American student," it said. "I am sorry, but I guess you'll have to take him."

To make matters worse, it became apparent that the decision to take me into their home wasn't unanimous. My hostess Pat, a matronly home economics teacher, had over-ruled her husband's objections and agreed to host "the American student" for a week so I wouldn't be on the street. But just for a week.

By the end of that week, I had made some friends and had offers galore of places to stay. Pat and her husband lifted the week-long limit, but I decided to move on to the home of some younger teachers. I was treated like a king.

For the remaining three months, the hospitality was non-stop. I hitchhiked from the northern to the southern tip of the country, staying with friends and relatives of teachers the whole way.

I hitched a ten-minute ride with one young couple. As they

dropped me off, they offered me the use of their house in Auckland. "We won't be home yet when you get there, but the key is under the mat, and the fridge is full."

Later in my trip, I finally asked why they had such trouble finding a place for me to stay before I arrived. It came out: Americans are seen by New Zealanders to be even less well-mannered than Australians.

"We wanted to make sure you were normal," one of the younger teachers said, as a way of apologizing for not offering a place to stay sooner. Turns out, a normal New Zealander is much like a normal Midwesterner: polite, generous, kind, gentle, but a little suspicious.

Most American tourists in New Zealand were obnoxious, more interested in talking loudly about their own country than in learning about the one they were visiting. Most of them, I learned on my travels, seemed to be from Texas, California or New York.

So, to these young professionals, allowing "an American student" into their home seemed akin to adopting a pet skunk.

But much to our mutual surprise, my small town Minnesota upbringing clicked well with the New Zealand outlook. I felt at home. They became comfortable with me. And they stopped demanding that I defend every American movie or government action.

Travel is good. It is not only good for us to see the world, but it is good for the world to see a picture of America besides what comes through the television set.

So do your patriotic duty, shy, polite citizens of Midwestern small towns: go overseas and be yourself. Be quiet. Listen. Learn. Talk softly, say thank you, and don't preach. By just being normal, you will shock a little part of the world.

CHAPTER FIVE

WORLD AFFAIRS

Sugar Beet Curriculum

A thought while driving through the rich green sugar beet fields of the Red River Valley: Why couldn't some enterprising high school develop an entire year-long curriculum based upon sugar beets?

Sugar beets are consistently the most profitable legal crop in the valley. The sugar industry employs thousands of area residents. The money from sugar dribbles down through our local economy in countless ways.

Why not toss out the dry, irrelevant textbooks and study this fascinating industry just outside our front door?

Far from being narrow in focus, the Sugar Beet Curriculum could be expanded to include most every academic discipline.

Chemistry students could study not only the farm chemicals and how they work, but the process by which sugar is processed. Botany students could study the growth cycle of the sugar beet, as well as the genetics of hybridizing new varieties.

The technology used in farming today is incredibly advanced. For example, Global Positioning Systems now steer tractors from outer space. The beet rows are straighter than ever, but a science student might ask: How does it all work?

Political Science students could study the politics of subsidies and tariffs, and the impact of national agriculture policies on our local area. Why, for instance, does the government always want low commodity prices? Why will farm states likely block any change in the Electoral College?

History students could study the farm co-op movement of the early to mid-1900s. What drove farmers to band together to build their own sugar beet plants, as well as grain elevators? Who opposed them? Why?

Why did the Communist Party gain a small but significant following amongst area farmers during the 1930s? How did World War II eliminate threshing machines in favor of combines? Why has the number of farmers gone from over 50% of the nation's population to under 3% in just one century?

Economics students could study the structure of the sugar cooperatives. Nothing closer to a centrally-planned economy exists in this country. Does it work? How can the beet plants thrive while the corn co-op got chewed up and swallowed by Cargill?

How do farmers respond to the tight restrictions placed on them by the cooperative? Isn't it un-American for somebody to tell you how many trucks you can use during harvest?

Ethics students could study the questions raised by genetically engineered crops. What are the implications of inserting codfish genes into plants? Does eating that stuff hurt you? Should Monsanto be able to prevent farmers from replanting their own seed?

Health students could study the allegedly sky-high cancer rates in rural northwestern Minnesota. Is cancer really more prevalent here? Is there any evidence that farm chemicals are to blame? Or do we just eat too much lefse and too little fiber?

American Literature students could read Louise Erdrich's novel "The Beet Queen." What does such a novel teach us about our area that science and statistics cannot?

Mathematics students could study the formulas used to calculate the payments made to beet farmers. How do they figure sugar content and dozens of other factors into the final figure? How do crop insurance companies use the highest forms of math to calculate their rates?

Of course, the students would take time off from school in October to work twelve-hour night shifts during beet harvest.

The Sugar Beet Curriculum could cover virtually every academic topic—except music. There are very few, if any, songs or ballads written about beet harvest. Perhaps the students, inspired by their experiences, would compose some.

Taxes

The snowplows were out late last week. They had no choice, of course, the roads were drifted, but if people could have just waited a couple of days for our sudden spring thaw, the whole mess would have melted off on its own, saving the county a little money in these financially difficult times.

The property tax notice came in the mail a couple of weeks ago. My house went up in value by a good chunk even though the only improvement I made in the past year was to clean the garage. I didn't think the garage was that messy, but it obviously was bad enough to hold my home value down several thousand dollars.

They will probably raise my property taxes, although I would never suspect that the county's cash crunch had anything to do with the increase in my home's assessed value. I am sure it was the clean garage.

But even if county taxes do go up, we get pretty good value for our county money. After a storm, the snowplows come by before I can even get out of bed in the morning. Most county roads are well-paved and well-maintained, and we need that.

Some property tax money goes to the school, which is a good thing. It stays in town. It is good for kids to learn. Other money goes towards county nursing, and everybody has good things to say about the county nurse who comes out once per month.

As for the state tax bill, we are told we live in a high tax state, but I am always impressed with how low the state tax bill is when it arrives. Again, all of that money is spent in the state. Nursing home aid is a good thing. We should take care of the weak and infirm, we should have good roads, and we should have nice schools. That's the Minnesota way.

The university gobbles up a good chunk of the money, which I wouldn't mind so much if the football team wasn't so bad. For all that money, you'd think they could win the Big 10 every now and then.

Granted, some university money goes to graduate students who write dissertations nobody will ever read. I can't complain about that since there is a thesis of mine written at North Dakota taxpayer's expense gathering dust somewhere. It contributed almost nothing to the sum total of human knowledge. However, the two years spent writing it were so much fun I would never deny the experience to somebody else for petty reasons of finance.

But it is the huge federal tax bill which gives me pause. You wonder which defense contractor is going to get it, in which case my contribution would probably purchase fifteen rivets, or if my money might go to some artist in Greenwich Village who paints pictures with elephant dung, or to some scientist at Berkeley who studies the mating patterns of gnats.

In reality, I suppose federal dollars roll back into the area about as fast they leave. As long as we keep having natural disaster after natural disaster, federal dollars will continue to help clean up the latest mess. And the feds are thoughtful enough to hire local people to run around quizzing farmers for those agriculture statistical reports nobody reads.

So, some of the money comes back to us from all the federal taxes we pay, as much as it feels like legalized robbery when one writes the check every spring.

Education Reform

Once again, the state of Minnesota is changing the rules for what children are supposed to learn in school. For the past couple of years, students had to put together a stack of projects in order to graduate. Now, apparently, they are going back to memorizing state capitols.

Looking back on my education, there are certain things which have come in more handy than others, and so I have some suggestions for state officials on this matter.

Multiplication is important. The multiplication table has stayed with me. We learned up to 12 x 12. To this day, if any number higher than thirteen gets thrown in, I have to get out a pad and pencil, or a calculator–but up to 12 x 12 I am fine. Thank you, taxpayers. Too bad the long division thing didn't work out.

Reading and writing have come in handy over the years. The dry textbooks of high school and college nearly killed the passion for reading I had as a sixth grader, but my interest revived after graduate school. Reading far outranks square dancing on the list of required skills I value most.

Yes, square dancing was required in Minnesota schools–at least into the 1980s. Not just any dancing, it had to be square dancing. It was the law. Or so our teacher told us when we complained bitterly about the two weeks of dosey-doeing.

A more useful element of the Physical Education curriculum was the seventeen weeks we spent each year learning the basics of dodgeball. I became an expert in dodgeball theory.

My main theory was to avoid getting plastered by one of the rifle-armed jocks by huddling in the corner with other kids who preferred to read.

As preparation for the corporate world, dodgeball should be required. Seventeen weeks per year should get the point across.

I haven't built another birdhouse since eighth grade, and a good thing for the birds. I got a C on that project, and that was due to charity on the part of the teacher. Birds refused to occupy it, and I burned it in a brief ceremony later that summer.

I once knew how to find the gonads on an earthworm. That piece of knowledge didn't stick past the test, but I can still smell the formaldehyde from Biology class. One should know what formaldehyde smells like so later on in life you can say "smells sort of like formaldehyde" and know what you're talking about.

We learned about glaciers and silts and loess and tarns and sediments and tectonic plates and igneous rock. But that's knowledge which, if you ever get to a part of the country where it matters, you can learn it from a plaque at the next rest area. Sort of a waste of taxpayer dollars to go over the material twice.

In tenth grade History class, we were required to learn the difference between Ionian and Doric carvings on columns of Greek and Roman temples. Very boring. But years later I found out what the Greeks and Romans were doing between the pillars of those temples. Much more interesting! Those details would have kept the class awake, and may even have increased the attendance at school board meetings.

Perhaps these small suggestions can be incorporated into the new set of educational requirements to be handed down by the state. If not, I'll just wait for the next governor and try again.

Terrorism through the Years

As astounding as last week's terrorist attacks were, what is even more astonishing is that it has taken this long for somebody to mount an attack on the American civilian population.

War on innocent civilians first became commonplace during World War II. Hitler killed millions of innocents in the nations he conquered. Stalin preferred to kill his own civilians, slaughtering Soviet ethnic minorities by the hundreds of thousands even as his military fought the Nazis.

The Allies were not innocent of killing civilians. The fire bombings of Dresden and Hamburg in 1945, two cities of little military consequence, killed nearly 100,000 civilians in two nights, most of them women, children and the elderly. The men were out of town, or already killed, fighting Hitler's war.

Churchill assented to those bombings for reasons which remain cloudy, but he had pangs of conscience. Killing civilians went against his 19th century gentlemanly ideals. When he saw the news reels of Dresden in flames, he suddenly yelled to those near him, "Have we become monsters?"

In addition to the dropping of the atomic bomb on Japan, the firebombing of suburban Tokyo killed as many as 100,000 people in almost as short a time. Again, mostly women, children and the elderly.

The war in Vietnam killed thousands of civilians, as did the more recent war in Iraq. By that time the killing of civilians was termed "collateral damage," and was seen as an unfortunate but necessary part of modern warfare.

Incredibly, during all of these conflicts, none of the countries we fought managed a terrorist attack on the American mainland of any consequence at all, much less an attack of the stupendous magnitude of that of September 11, 2001.

There has been death on the American mainland. The tremendous carnage of the Civil War killed nearly 500,000 Americans, including tens of thousands in single days. But nearly all casualties were soldiers. Civilians, with a few exceptions, were spared.

The unprecedented devastation of last week's attacks must have surprised even the surviving conspirators. Nobody imagined the World Trade Center towers would collapse as completely as if they had been planted with explosives by a skilled demolition team.

But this method of terror–ramming commercial planes into large buildings–was a one shot deal, made obsolete only minutes after it happened by events in the sky over Pennsylvania.

I suspect the passengers in the Pennsylvania plane were in a state of shock and disbelief when they were hijacked, inclined to sit still like we are always told to and not provoke the lunatics who took over the plane.

But that was before those passengers heard on their cell phones that only minutes earlier, other hijacked planes had struck buildings full of people. After those calls, at least some passengers realized that not only were they doomed, but thousands more might die if they didn't do something quick.

They did something, we don't know exactly what. But only minutes after learning of this new level of terror, the passengers acted on the fresh facts and took desperate action to save the lives of others.

Perhaps terrorists are smart enough to realize that, with last week's horrible episode in the back of their minds, future hijacked passengers won't likely sit still and remain calm.

Churchill's Courage

If terrorists continue to disrupt our domestic tranquility, we can look to history for examples of people who have coped with similar problems.

From September 7 to November 3 of 1940, a space of fifty-seven days, over 200 German bombers attacked London, England every night. Daytime attacks were common as well. Thousands perished.

Winston Churchill urged the British citizens to go about their work each day, even as the bombing continued. The populace did so cheerfully.

When bombs hit a factory, as they did almost daily, the dead and wounded were taken away, the debris cleared, repairs made, and the factory began production again, often within hours.

The attack on England was an attempt by Hitler to subdue the British people. He hoped to damage Britain's economy, but most of all he hoped to destroy British morale through sheer terror.

Morale was low early on, but the pugnacious new prime minister rallied the citizens. "We will fight them on the beaches," Churchill said, although he added later to an aide: "We will have to hit them over the head with beer bottles, because that is all we have."

Churchill used every device he could muster to infuse the British with courage. British antiaircraft guns were useless at night, but Churchill ordered blanks fired in the air so the people would think something was being done.

After nightfall, Churchill often sent his servants and aides down to the shelter, grabbed a cigar and a bottle of champagne, and went up to the roof to watch what he called "the grand show." His gallant example inspired British citizens to take incredible daily risks.

The Brits developed a dark humor as they went about their work.

When the Germans spread land mines all over the England, thousands of volunteer groups formed to disarm the mines. The most famous such group consisted of the Earl of Suffolk, his chauffeur and the Earl's elderly secretary.

Most groups disabled a dozen mines or so before they goofed and were blown up. But the Earl and his two servants were unusually skillful. The Holy Trinity, as they called themselves due to their longevity, diffused an incredible thirty-four mines.

They finally slipped up on number thirty-five, however. As an admiring Churchill put it in his memoirs, "Up went the Earl of Suffolk with his Holy Trinity."

Tough times, courageous people, great stories. But the tale of Churchill on the roof watching the bombs fall has taken a recent twist.

In the 1980s, it was revealed that the British knew the German secret radio codes for most of the war. Even though he could do nothing about the attacks, Churchill usually knew where the Luftwaffe planned to hit each night.

An energetic historian went to work with this new information a couple of years ago. With some good detective work, he figured out that on the nights the Germans planned to hit Churchill's neighborhood, there were no champagne and cigars on the roof. On those nights, Winston was deep in the bunker.

Bach

At the finish of a Bach piece played on Minnesota Public Radio last week, the velvet-voiced host observed: "After a Bach piece, it is possible to think all is well with the world."

This past September 12, a cellist who lived near the World Trade Center set out carrying his instrument and a folding chair towards the smoldering wreckage of the twin towers. Guards let him through the barricades. The musician set up within earshot of resting rescue workers, where he played Bach's mournful Suite for Unaccompanied Cello.

Only the music of Johann Sebastian Bach could appear at such a place, at such a time, and seem not only appropriate, but enriching and uplifting.

With 100 channels of television, the Internet, radio and newspapers, it is possible—even out here in the woods during this charmed season, miles from anything that matters—to feel overwhelmed by the sadness of world affairs.

There soon comes a time to switch off the modern gadgets which funnel the troubles of the world into one's living room, and turn on a modern gadget which can soothe one's soul, a stereo. More specifically, a stereo tuned to the music of Bach.

One can drift off into other musical regions—into the lighthearted brilliance of Mozart, the demogogic bombast of Beethoven, the ragged rawness of the Rolling Stones, the twanging pangs of Hank Williams, Sr., or the mind-numbing vapidity of modern pop—but when an existential funk looms, it's back to Bach.

A picture is worth a thousand words, but great music speaks volumes. In fact, it is difficult to describe great music without coming across as pompous and pretentious. (Please refer to the previous paragraph.)

But I must try. Everybody knows some Bach. His music shows up in video games, on pinball machines, in television commercials, in movies, on cell phone ringers, at weddings. You can't miss it. It's everywhere.

Bach died in 1750. For the next seventy years, his music languished unplayed in his attic. One of Bach's sons sold about half of the sheets for fishwrap to support his beer-drinking habit.

Once his music was rediscovered, Bach's astounding genius became apparent. Today, his music is played well, played badly, played to sell toothpaste, played to scare movie goers, played at state funerals and royal weddings, played on every instrument from the bowunga to the bassoon, all over the world.

You can listen to a Bach piece hundreds of times, even play one from memory, without hearing or understanding all that is going on—yet, that same piece can charm a child. When performed well by warm-hearted and thoughtful musicians, the music of Bach leaves one with that same content feeling you get from downing a plateful of fluffy mashed potatoes.

But words fail. Purchase a Bach recording. My favorite disc at present is Stowkoski's Symphonic Bach, recorded by the BBC Orchestra. Listen to the recording twenty times. If you are not enriched by the old man's music, send the recording to me. The day I receive it, I will drop a crisp twenty in the mail to you, enclosed in a sympathy card.

TV News

Watching the news too much, especially these days, can turn one into a paranoid, nervous wreck. News watching is a habit as destructive to one's mental health as drinking, smoking, coffee, soap operas, bad novels, shopping, and other unhealthy compulsions.

The news the networks dish out on a daily basis is pure trash. Their whole goal, it seems, is to keep the populace's paranoia at a fever pitch. You could be next! Here's what you can do! No wonder you have senior citizens in Sunny Park Retirement Home in Podunk, MN not opening their mail for fear they are the target of terrorists.

Real news seldom seeps in. Seventeen people might get massacred in Israel, but you won't hear about that unless you watch the BBC. No, our networks are too busy whipping the American people up into a frenzy over powder in envelopes.

Paranoia keeps ratings up, and revenues drive network news more than anything. Truth has little to do with it.

Conservative commentator Bill Maher learned that. The host of late night TV's *Politically Incorrect* recently made the mistake of stating a truth obvious to a child of five: flying an airplane into a building, certainly an insane and evil act, takes more courage than it does to push a button which sends a missile into a target hundreds of miles away.

You'd think Maher had come out for flag burning. Several stations canceled his show. The White House spokesman told him to "watch what you say," not just now, but all the time.

Other journalists blasted him.

Worst of all, Maher started to lose advertisers. That did it. Maher, whose statement was an attempt to clarify what is meant by the word cowardice, became a coward himself. He apologized for his statement in a last-ditch effort to rescue his show.

No, the truth doesn't matter in news these days, especially if it is unpopular. If your news show is paid for by advertisers and you start stating uncomfortable truths, it won't be long before you don't have a news show. Corporations selling toothpaste aren't into courage.

What matters for news people is that you find the bandwagon of the moment and jump on it. That will keep the sponsors happy, and the White House off your back. Trouble is, the bandwagon can change directions in a hurry, and usually does.

The thirst for revenge will fade, the war effort could bog down, the American people will have little tolerance for American casualties, and popular sentiment may well abandon our president as quickly as it once gathered around him.

And the network newspersons, who wanted to throw bombs at everything a month ago, will do nothing to stand in the way of the wild swings of popular opinion, however wrong they are.

The popular opinions of the moment are likely to be those which make people feel most entertained, titillated, fearful and anxious–for it is those emotions which keep people glued to the tube, propping up network ratings, instead of out tilling their garden or cleaning their gutters.

Wars

The wars fought by this country in its history cross the entire spectrum, from the noble and memorable on one end, to the ignoble and forgettable on the other.

The Civil War is remembered as the struggle to preserve the Union and free the slaves. It was the most violent war in the world's history at the time, with tens of thousands dying each day of battle. It was begun and waged, with utter agony, by a humble and humane man, Abraham Lincoln, who, despite his resolute public face, searched his soul during the long, dark nights of the war, wondering if he was in the right, weighing the horrible human cost of battle against the larger principles at stake.

World War II is also well-remembered. Few question the nobility of the Allied cause. That war brought forth two great leaders, Winston Churchill and Dwight Eisenhower, who, despite their conviction that they were in the right and their determination to win, never lost sight of the horrible human cost of the fighting.

As he watched newsreels of the Allied bombing of civilian Dresden, Churchill stood up and shouted, "Have we become monsters?" He had deep doubts, and they are to his credit.

Eisenhower's dread of sending young men into combat drove him to smoke four packs of filterless Pall Malls per day. When he accepted honors after the war, he reminded his admirers in eloquent terms that he did so only on behalf of those who died due to his decisions.

Both wars were epic conflicts. The outcome was uncertain, but the consequences of not fighting were clear–and the results, however imperfect, have stood the test of time.

At the other end of the spectrum are two forgotten conflicts, the Mexican War and the Spanish-American War. Both were lopsided affairs in which victory was never in doubt. Both were started with great acclaim by men whom history has largely forgotten, Presidents James K. Polk and William McKinley. Neither Polk nor McKinley regarded war itself with anything more than a shrug.

The Mexican War ended in a great grab of territory by the United States, territory which today includes much of the American Southwest. The Spanish-American War ended with the United States in control of Cuba and the Phillipines.

In both cases, the American public was lathered up for war by the alleged threat the enemy posed to the United States, as well as the corruption and brutality of their rule. But no matter the motive, territory was the most lasting result.

Quick and easy American victories didn't improve matters in the long-term for the conquered countries. After many regime changes, Cuba ended up with Castro, and the Phillipines wound up with decades of rule by the murderous Marcos.

Perhaps for those reasons, the Mexican and Spanish-American Wars have been largely swept under history's rug. No documentaries on PBS trumpet the virtues of the presidents who started them. No epic battles inspired legends, songs or poetry.

To be remembered with pride, it seems, a war's purpose must be clear. Those who begin it must forcefully disavow and forbid less-than-noble motives such as profit and territory. The threat prevented must have been real, and the freedom brought to the liberated must be actual and lasting.

In addition, it seems apparent that leaders who go to war, if they wish to be remembered kindly by history or remembered at all, must do so with soberness, humility, and a deep and sincere reluctance.

Lincoln

Abraham Lincoln's reputation as a saintly martyr arose within hours of his death and has obscured reality ever since. The Lincoln legend contains some truth, but its growth was shaped by the politics of the time.

At the time of his assassination, many Northern politicians and much of the populace worried Lincoln was going too easy on the defeated South. They much preferred to wring the Confederacy's neck. Newspapers called for the hanging of traitors by the thousand.

The Sunday after Lincoln died, prominent preachers in Northern pulpits echoed the general feeling that the meek Lincoln was removed from the scene by God to allow divine retribution against the South to flow more freely. He was a saint, but his mission was complete.

Even Lincoln's staunchest enemies in the North eulogized him as a simple, pious man, martyred by the desperate and evil slave holders. No harm praising the dead, they seemed to think. More important, the murder of such a harmless man only proved that the South deserved whatever rough treatment came its way.

But Abe Lincoln was not simple, nor was he particularly pious. In fact, he was the shrewdest of politicians. He was our greatest president by a large margin, but for complicated reasons long shrouded in myth.

The Emancipation Proclamation provides a good example. With that eloquent document, Lincoln declared the slaves to be free. His great words were destined to be etched in history books and on granite walls across the nation.

But a close reading shows that the Proclamation freed only slaves in territory held by the South. In other words, because Lincoln had no authority over those areas, the Proclamation freed absolutely nobody. Furthermore, it kept in bondage thousands of slaves in territory held by the Northern armies.

Historians still struggle to figure out Lincoln's motives. Some say he merely hoped that the Emancipation Proclamation would cause the Southern-held slaves to rise up. Others note that Northern enthusiasm for preserving the Union was waning as the battles grew more bloody. The Emancipation provided a much-needed higher purpose to justify the war's carnage.

Yet others have found evidence that Lincoln hoped the noble words of the Proclamation would arouse wild enthusiasm in the lower classes of Europe, which would pressure European monarchs to quit supporting the South. In fact, much to Lincoln's satisfaction, this happened.

Lincoln could have issued the Emancipation Proclamation on his first day in office. That he waited to do so until the idea became strategically useful, and applied it only where it would cause the enemy trouble, speaks volumes.

The Proclamation and countless other examples show Lincoln to be more a brilliant lawyer than a moral crusader.

And Lincoln was a brilliant lawyer. In frontier Illinois, he was a legend. If you killed a man in cold blood, Abe Lincoln was the lawyer who could get you off, either on a technicality, or by convincing the jury that the other guy deserved it.

Known to history as a placid and merciful gentleman, Lincoln was famous on the Illinois frontier as a wrestler and fist fighter, perhaps the toughest in the state.

Known to history as a martyr for a holy cause, Lincoln's early statements on religion reveal a testy agnosticism which only later mellowed.

Known to history as a comical storyteller, Lincoln frequently descended into depressions so deep that friends considered him suicidal.

The misty idealism which causes us to celebrate Lincoln's birthday as a national holiday is appropriate. Lincoln was one of the greats. But like many of the greats, he has been frequently, and often completely, misunderstood.

Monsters and Presidents

Violence in movies and television gets blamed for all sorts of societal ills. Who knows who is at fault, the studios which make the junk, the masses who pay to see it, or if any of it matters at all.

I am more offended by children's cartoons. Have you ever stopped to watch these kid's shows which everybody thinks are so harmless?

When cartoons come on, kids sit mesmerized in front of the TV as if they are on tranquilizers. Good enough, many parents think, as they slip into the next room for a little peace and quiet.

Meanwhile, the cartoon characters bash each other over the head with sledge hammers, shoot each other with shotguns and push each other off mile-high cliffs. And nobody ever gets hurt!

You might think a Disney cartoon would be a safe bet for kids. But when the folks at Disney decide to make an evil character, they really make them evil. I watched part of Riki Tiki Tavi the other night, and even a cartoon cobra gave me the creeps.

For that matter, I think some of the classic children's stories are pretty bad, too. Wolves trying to eat little girls. Wicked step-mothers. Evil witches. Hans Christian Anderson didn't seem to care how many nightmares he caused.

I recently babysat a four-year-old, and we read storybooks. The evil characters were truly scary. To her credit, the little girl knew when the next evil character was coming, and she quickly covered that part of the page up with her hands so neither of us would get nightmares.

These stories were Sleeping Beauty, Little Red Riding Hood, Cinderella and the like, not some modern super-hero dramas.

Perhaps I am a freak. I grew up in a household with no television, no scary fairy tales, just lots of history books. I never saw enough TV to grow numb to it.

When our family stayed in motels, we kids naturally wanted to soak in all the TV we could. But my mother forbade us to watch violent cartoons. I thought at the time that Mom just wanted the TV to herself so she could watch Carol Burnett. Now I see her point.

But those stacks of history books had their problems, too. I remember one which contained a picture of Abe Lincoln that scared me to the bone. Something about that sad stare and his long, crossed legs gave me chills.

That picture was in my favorite book on presidents. So, when I got to James K. Polk, I would grab a ream of pages and turn the whole bunch so I didn't have to glimpse that scary picture of Abe Lincoln.

Just to be safe, I usually jumped all the way forward to Rutheford B. Hayes. That was when I was in second grade. To this day I know virtually nothing about Andrew Johnson or Ulysses Grant, all because I didn't want to get stared down by Honest Abe.

Manchester

For years I have been awaiting the third volume of William Manchester's biography of Winston Churchill. Manchester's first two volumes were masterful, but the third volume was to encompass World War II, when Churchill truly shone.

Manchester's writing is informative, but also good and gossipy. He puts in all the juicy details. For instance, he devotes a whole chapter in his second volume to Churchill's odd habits.

Churchill started drinking when he awoke, at about noon, and didn't stop until he went to bed at 4:00 a.m. He wrote 56 books in his lifetime, penning nearly all of his dazzling prose between 11 p.m. and bedtime. During those hours, he generally switched from gin to champagne.

From age sixteen on, Churchill's valet dressed him every morning. The same servant also toweled him off after his bath. He knew Churchill was done bathing when he heard the honorable gentleman turn a somersault in the bathtub, blowing bubbles as his head went under the water.

If you want more great gossip, find Manchester's biography in a bookstore and read the first chapter of the second volume. That chapter contains some of the finest historical writing I have ever run across.

Needless to say, I have been looking forward to reading Manchester's interpretation of Churchill's performance as British prime minister during the war. Churchill wrote his side of the story, over 3,000 pages worth of wonderful reading, but you have to take it with a grain of salt.

Well, I found out last week why Manchester has never completed the final volume of Churchill's biography. He had a stroke, after which he fully recovered his physical powers. But when Manchester tried to write again, he could not. The sentences did not come.

At age seventy-nine, after years of hoping his abilities would return, William Manchester, our greatest living historian, has been forced to give up on his most ambitious project. His biographies of H. L. Mencken, Gen. Douglas MacArthur and John F. Kennedy remain classics, but the Churchill biography was to have been his crowning achievement.

Manchester fought under MacArthur in the Pacific during World War II. However, the first biography he wrote upon his return from the war was of the great American writer and critic, H. L. Mencken. Mencken was Manchester's hero, and is one of my heroes as well.

Now the rest of the story: soon after Manchester started his research, Mencken had a stroke which took away his ability to read and write. Young Manchester visited Mencken frequently. His purpose was to ask questions about Mencken's life. Mencken could still talk.

But soon young Manchester realized that Mencken longed more than anything for somebody to read to him. Manchester read aloud to Mencken for hundreds of hours over the space of several years, until the old curmudgeon finally died.

Now, through a sad twist of fate, Manchester finds himself in the same sorry state as Mencken in his last years.

Let's hope some young student is reading books aloud to old William Manchester. Sometimes it's only right and good that what goes around comes around.

The Old Days

Drastic change continues to roll across the countryside of Minnesota with quiet but irresistible force. The harsh winds of economic reality have ruthlessly felled the rugged old ways, old buildings, and old institutions into streamlined modern swaths.

Isolated pockets of resistance hold out. A few country churches struggle on, although the number of cars outside no longer requires latecomers to park nose-in-the-ditch unless there is a meatball supper or a funeral.

Some sagging barns remain, but only as relics. Dairy cattle have moved on to the bovine equivalent of suburban apartment buildings, huge computerized dairies so hidden that even rural children might be excused for thinking their milk comes from a factory.

Farm machinery has become so efficient that the planting and harvest of the quarter section next door can happen in one afternoon. The people in the tractors might live twenty miles away. You still wave at them, if you happen to be around the day they sweep across the field, but that doesn't mean you know who they are.

Not that long ago each quarter section supported a teeming farmyard of kids, animals, rickety outbuildings, and noisy year-round bustle.

County fairs, originally meant to encourage farm kids to show their first attempts at raising animals and crops, or for their mothers to show off their jellies and jams, have had to adapt to modern entertainment demands or simply shut down.

And yet, despite this seeming tragedy, nostalgia for the old days isn't universal amongst the locals, and it tends to be confined to people such as myself who didn't have to live through the old days themselves.

Some old-timers express sadness and say, "Things aren't like they used to be," or "We were poor, but we were happy." Yet the stories of others, less often told, make it clear that the past was no picnic.

For example, increased openness has made it seem as if problems such as alcoholism, domestic abuse, depression, and other social and personal problems are recent developments. However, it is obvious that such evils always existed, but were simply shoved under the rug.

What hope did an abused wife have fifty years ago? An alcoholic? Somebody struggling with depression? It is easy to say that back then people were tougher, and maybe they were, but you don't have to dig very deeply to hear stories of deep and unabated suffering.

Memory's filter often sifts out the good and discards the bad. It is easier that way, and probably for the best. But I have come to understand why not every old-timer laments the passing of the old days and ways.

Times were tough. The poverty was often grinding. The tight community ties of the old days had their good side, and may seem idyllic to those of us appalled by modern isolation, but those ties arose out of a continual struggle to survive, and didn't allow for much privacy or individual difference.

The past was both better and worse than the present. I am for preserving as much of it as possible, including the old barns, old churches and old schoolhouses—not because the loss of the old ways is a tragedy, but because the old days and ways can teach us how fortunate we are today, and at the same time show us what we are missing.

Wellstone

In July of 1990, soon after Paul Wellstone was nominated by the DFL to run against Rudy Boschwitz for the U. S. Senate, he stopped by the Polk County Fair in Fertile, MN.

It was too early in the day for a good crowd at the fairgrounds. I was working selling plants. Business was slow for me, and Wellstone could find almost nobody to talk to on the grounds but his own staffer and editor of the local paper.

I knew nothing about Wellstone except that his politics were way off in left field, he didn't look at all like a senator, and he probably didn't stand a chance against Rudy Boschwitz's millions. The consensus at the time was that Wellstone got the nomination because nobody respectable wanted it.

I decided to go shake his hand. Wellstone was friendly, of course, but so short and funny looking that I didn't feel uncomfortable asking him in a somewhat disrespectful tone, "So, what makes you think you can pull this off?"

Wellstone laughed. He seemed happy to have an audience. He launched into one of his trademark sermons on the spot, brow furrowed, arms going up and down, finger jabbing the air.

He knew he was the underdog, he said, but money wasn't everything and gosh, Eric, do you know what's going on in this country? Corporations are taking over the farms. People are going without health care. Small towns are dying.

I was a smart-aleck college student selling petunias for the summer, an audience of one, but Wellstone kept going as if I was a jam-packed convention hall. Eventually he paused and asked me what I thought. How would you run against Boschwitz? Do you think I can win?

I am sure I said nothing coherent in response, but I was charmed.

Wellstone brimmed with enthusiasm for causes which can seem so hopeless, so tired. Plus, he had asked my advice on how to run his campaign.

As a freshman Senator, Wellstone made some unfortunate errors. He used the Vietnam Memorial as a backdrop to protest the Gulf War, infuriating veterans' groups. He used a White House reception to hand the first President Bush a stack of videos of citizens opposed to his policies. He stated that he "despised" right-wing Senator Jesse Helms.

But only two years later, he received a "Legislator of the Year" award from several veterans' groups for his advocacy of veterans' causes. And after Wellstone's death in last week's tragic plane crash, Jesse Helms would say tearfully of his colleague that, "He was my friend, and I was his."

Wellstone grew on the job, and won the admiration of people who opposed his every idea. His earnestness was inexhaustible. His enthusiasm was infectious.

But Wellstone's most lasting legacy will be with the thousands of ordinary people–college students, cleaning ladies, security guards, waitresses, farmers–he made feel important by treating them with the same dignity and importance as if they were the President of the United States.

Wellstone loved the regular people, and they loved him back. They hugged him and even patted him on the head. They called him Paul.

Yes, so good was Wellstone at making the little people feel important that when I woke up the day after Election Day 1990 to the news that Wellstone had indeed pulled off a victory, part of me thought that our little talk that summer might have been the turning point.

Election Speech

I would just like to thank you all for your support last Tuesday. I couldn't have done it without you. Your many kindnesses throughout the campaign have touched both myself and I very deeply.

Thank you for tolerating my campaign's advertisements. I know they were an insult to the intelligence of anybody with a brain larger than a frog's. But most elections are decided by the frog-brain swing vote, so what can you do? Get down there in the mud, I say.

Thank you for believing that my opponent is the devil incarnate. He's actually a nice guy, now that he's defeated, but we felt we needed to bring up the womanizing thing, even though we have no evidence. Did you see him squirm? Could have been something to the charges after all, in which case my campaign provided a valuable public service to his wife.

Thank you for believing that if elected I will provide free prescription drugs to all seniors, as well as juniors and sophomores. I have a few boxes of free samples in my office. Stop by and we'll fix you up.

As for my promise to save the family farm, I'll get right on it. According to my staff, the lone remaining family farm is somewhere southeast of Grand Forks, and we are determined to save it if it takes a million sandbags.

I will also be revitalizing rural communities. We'll be going from town to town with a John Deere Revitalizer 4650, which looks a lot like one of those big fertilizer spreaders. The revitalization should allow us to squeeze about five or ten more bushels-per-acre out of the grain planted in our small-town industrial parks.

I must take a brief moment to acknowledge my opponent's efforts to convince small towns to plant crops in their industrial parks rather than letting them grow up in weeds. This brilliant revenue-generating scheme represents a major paradigm shift and has been replicated with success in small town industrial parks throughout the Upper Midwest.

Rest assured, I will never waver in my commitment to traditional values. Nothing beats traditional values–like two for the price of one, double coupons, senior discounts, or buy one get one free. These time-honored values must be upheld and passed on!

I continue to believe that our children are our future. Scary thought, but it's true. We need to invest in our future! Schools must be adequately funded. That means heat and lights, and enough computers to keep the brats so busy playing games that they don't riot.

In fact, it is critically important that our children remain completely mesmerized by electronic devices in those crucial years before they join the workforce and finally make themselves useful. Just remember, a child clutching a bag of Doritoes in front of a television set is not joining a gang or doing drugs!

As for teachers, I firmly believe that all three of them should be well-paid. And they must be given the tools they need to do their jobs, be it handcuffs, chains, stun-guns, tear gas, whatever. We must not shortchange the future.

I will continue to be unabashedly in favor of choice. Nobody should tell others what to do! And I am in favor of life, too. Where would we be without it?

Yes, I look forward to serving you, my constituents, these next years. Wherever you may go, you can count on me taking the credit for leading you there.

Waylon

After hearing last week that Waylon Jennings had died, I stuck one of his greatest hits albums in my pickup's CD player. It will probably be there for a while.

Waylon Jennings and Willie Nelson introduced me to country music in the late seventies. Country music wasn't cool at the time, but Waylon and Willie broke through to kids like myself who would never have been caught dead listening to George Jones, Conway Twitty or even Johnny Cash.

Somebody loaned me a tape of Waylon and Willie, and I wore it out before I could give it back. A solo cassette of Waylon's met the same fate.

Obituaries of Waylon make a lot of his outlaw image and his bucking of the so-called country music establishment. He and Willie were supposedly big rebels, and that image is what made them famous.

That's bunk. Waylon and Willie were simply authentic. People sense authenticity. The public is always hungry for it. David Letterman, a big Waylon fan, always introduced him as "the real deal," a sincere compliment from an expert in fakes.

No shiny suits, plastic hair or cheesy stage acts for Waylon and Willie. Just music, and some of the very best country music possible. They succeeded because they could sing like nobody else.

Willie Nelson's twang is more famous, and easy to imitate. Just plug your nose and warble. But nobody even tries to imitate Waylon's tobacco-rich baritone. It is his alone, a wonderful voice mellowed by years of hard living.

Take the country ballad "Amanda," one of Waylon's greatest hits. When he sings the line, "I looked in the mirror in total surprise, at the hair on my shoulders, the age in my eyes," it gets me every time. Authentic. The real deal. Sung from deep down. Melancholy, but not maudlin.

Of course, you always wonder what these guys are like in person. I mean, would you buy a used car from George Jones? Hank Williams Jr. seems angry and out of control. Wouldn't care to meet him. And nobody has ever accused Willie Nelson of being a gentleman.

By his own admission, Waylon spent 21 years high on cocaine, up to fifteen hundred dollars worth per day. Jessie Colter was his fourth wife. Nobody is saying what happened to the first three. Perhaps we don't want to know.

But I have always thought there was something gentle and big-hearted about Waylon. He sang with the tough tenderness of a grizzled cowboy holding his newborn first grandchild.

Waylon and Jessie were together for the last 32 years, apparently happy. In 1984, Waylon quit cocaine. By the end of his life, he seems to have tackled his demons. He seemed content for reasons deeper than fame.

I suppose we trip over ourselves to find virtue in celebrities we admire, especially when they have just died. But I am going to allow myself to think Waylon Jennings was the real deal. Nobody fake could sing like that, could they?

CHAPTER SIX

SCIENCE AND NATURE

Equinox

The spring equinox happens this week, when the axis of the earth's rotation lines up exactly perpendicular to the sun.

On March 21, just as on September 21, the entire planet has exactly twelve hours of day and twelve hours of night. Then for the next six months, we in the northland will have more hours of sunshine than anybody south of us.

The ancients carefully observed the natural calendar. They had little else to do for fun. They had no TV to keep them hypnotized, no city lights to dim the stars at night, no other way to keep track of the seasons but by what they saw in nature.

Even in our modern world, there are ways for the observant to keep in touch with celestial rhythms.

In this flat part of the country, most roads align with the compass. At equinox, the sun sets right at the end of the highway going west. Westbound traffic should prepare to be blinded at sunset this week.

Of course, the sun rises right at the end of the eastbound highways at equinox, too, but that happens in the morning when sensible people like myself are still asleep.

I once lived in a trailer house which was perfectly aligned with the compass. On the evening of the equinox, and only on the equinox, a narrow beam of sunshine traveled through the back window, down the hall, through the living room, past the kitchen—and cast a dim, orange spot on the otherwise dark wall of the dining room, 72 feet away.

In ancient times, people marked the equinox with a party for the neighbors. They danced around the bonfire with rattles until sunrise, at which time they ran back into their trailers to catch the beam of sunshine going down the hall the opposite way. It was quite an event.

Nowadays, plants notice March 21 more keenly than people do. For some reason, Morning Glory will bloom three times as much in climates where they reach the two-leaf stage a week before equinox, when the days are still shorter than the nights.

Morning Glory germinate in May up here, missing the deadline. University researchers have found that you can trick the plants into thinking they germinated before March 21 by covering them with a bushel basket for a few hours per day during the two-leaf stage. The result? Triple the bloom come summer.

Junebearing strawberries notice June 22, the first day of the year which is shorter than the previous one. They stop forming blooms that very day. The same researchers who figured out the Morning Glory problem used artificial light to fool strawberries into thinking the days were getting longer all summer. Sure enough, the plants bloomed and bore until frost.

Humans in the modern world are tuned to other calendars. The start of baseball season is a big one for me. Others wait for the fishing opener.

But tuning into the celestial calendar every now and then might be a good idea. What better way to remind ourselves of the utter inconsequentiality of our daily worries?

Signs of Spring

Last week, spring arrived all at once in northern Minnesota. I believe it was last Thursday afternoon, April 11, that the weather finally fell into line with what the weather wizards have been predicting for weeks.

Temperatures suddenly soared into the lower 60s. Within the next day, the ice on the lakes darkened to a greenish blue. A few tender strands of grass appeared on the south side of the house.

The mud in the driveway quickly began to firm up. Soon it will be possible to walk all the way into the fridge with your work boots on without leaving a trail of mud chunks on the white linoleum. Another important spring milestone.

Earlier last week, I had hauled what I hoped would be the last load of wood. That pile of ash was burning up fast—until Thursday's warm-up. That night, I set the six remaining logs off to the side. They'll sit there until October.

Friday morning I heard the chattery song of the red-winged blackbird for the first time this season. That same afternoon, the first frogs clucked and croaked down in the swamp.

Then there is that bird that climbs up to altitudes so high that you can barely pick it out—and then goes into a dive. The bird's call gets louder and faster as it gains speed, tapering off as it pulls up. Do-do-do-DO-DO-DO-do-doop is about the best description of the call I can come up with on paper.

I don't know what the bird looks like, and I have no idea

what it is called, but its distant call has been a bittersweet sign of the April warm-up for me since childhood. I heard that bird for the first time this season last Saturday at dusk.

Friday also brought the first motorcycle sightings since last November. I spotted a big flock of Harley's just north of Fargo, the first of the season. What a racket they make as they gather around the watering hole. Honda's and Yamaha's don't tend to flock up like the Harley's do, but one or two can sometimes be seen flitting around a couple of days after the Harley's appear.

Yes, with these long-awaited signs of spring we no longer need to be jealous of those blasted cousins in Ohio or Georgia who gloat over the phone about their blooming Bradford pear, redbuds and dogwoods—while we sit trapped in the utter drab of a Minnesota March.

Reports of temperatures in the 70s in southern Indiana in March can make a Minnesotan bitter. Why must we righteous northerners suffer while the morally degenerate people of southern climes bask in undeserved sunshine?

But after spring came last Thursday, we can say that it is our turn. The southern climes have had their fun. As Arizona's temperatures climb into triple digits and the humidity in other parts south nears body temperature, we in northern Minnesota can relish another few weeks of perfect working-in-the-woods weather.

We'll know the fun is over when we feel the tickle of that first tick, or hear the whine of an incoming mosquito.

Hearing the Birds

What we wouldn't do in mid-winter for one day of weather as perfect as we had last week. But if one isn't careful, these sterling late-summer days can slip by underappreciated and even unnoticed.

Back when video cameras were a new thing, my aunt and uncle from California stopped by the farm for a visit. They ran around the yard taking video, and later we all got to watch ourselves on television, a big thrill at the time.

What we all noticed was not how fat we looked on video, or how strange our voices sounded, but how many birds there were singing in the background. They were loud, there were lots of them— and not one of us recalled hearing them during the filming.

Pretty crazy, I thought later, that it took two electronic machines—a camera and a television—before we finally took notice of the birds that chirp around us every day.

Now I occasionally remember to listen to the birds in the summer. Live birds, not ones on tape. After all, it gets pretty quiet outside in January. It makes sense to enjoy the birds while they are here.

A few years later, I went to the movie "Grumpy Old Men." It was filmed in Minnesota, during the winter. The scenery on the film was beautiful, I thought. Snowbanks, ice on the lakes, icicles hanging from the eaves.

Then, I realized that the scenery in the movie was the same drab stuff I complain so bitterly about those long winter months. When those same winter scenes were splashed on the silver screen, my attitude changed.

In August, each day is filled with things to watch, smell, hear and taste. Corn on the cob. Fresh tomatoes. Birds. Thunderstorms. Flowers. Green grass. A Twins team in first place. All the things we miss in the winter.

Yet one's mind can get so cluttered with petty daily worries that all of these good things which are smack dab in front of us fade into the background. Wasn't Alice a bit abrupt on the phone? Who will I get to shingle the roof? Am I ever going to be able to afford a new car?

Technology makes our mental busyness worse. Just when things settle down, the phone rings. A quiet moment? Better check my email for the twentieth time today. Oops, five minutes till my favorite show.

But the best show going is the one that is around us each day: the flowers blooming, the birds singing, the combines grinding away in the field, the deer nibbling on the petunias, the barnswallows dive-bombing mosquitoes.

My guess is that we'd all be better off if we took greater notice of the fascinating things going on around us rather than getting our stimulation from the tube, the silver screen, the internet, or the cell phone.

Noisy modern life with its gadgets dulls our senses, distracts us, agitates us, tempts us, removes our minds so far from the present moment that if the Garden of Eden itself were to pop up in our midst, few people would notice. They are, after all, expecting an important call.

June Memories

June in the northland is a time of bright greens. This is what we have waited for for the past seven months: green grass, breezes through open windows, fresh leaves on the trees, chattering birds.

Dusk lasts until just before eleven in the evening, and the sun rises well before most people make use of it. With the last snows still fresh in our mind, it is difficult to comprehend that the days will soon start getting shorter.

Is there anything more dreamlike and melancholy than a cloudy June afternoon? The farm fields are lush and silent, like massive fairways. The blooms of old lilacs, spireas and roses make their annual appearance in the brush on abandoned farm places, making one wonder who planted them and when.

Each June brings back the bittersweet loneliness of childhood summers. I lived too far from my school friends to see them during the summer, except for summer sports or the county fair.

Summer was a time for cousins, some of whom would visit the farm for weeks on end. It seemed like every week a strange station wagon would pull up to the house. An uncle would get out and stretch, an aunt would bustle into the house with pans of goodies, and cousins would pile out onto the lawn.

To pass the summer days, I used a lopping shears to clear trails through the woods for my little motorcycle. The trails were rough at first, but when the city cousins came, they rode the trails from morning till night until the paths were worn smooth.

Later on, the three-wheeler was the toy of choice. The best time to drive was at sunset when you could feel the mosquitoes pelting your face, or drink in the heavy cool air where the field roads dipped into a swampy hollow.

June was time to capture a bottle full of lightning bugs and let them light up my bedroom for a couple of nights before they started to stink.

June was when Rod Carew would be flirting with .400, and the Twins still had hope. Larry Hisle, Lyman Bostock, Roy Smalley, Glenn Adams and other long-forgotten Minnesota boys of summer played like all-stars in June. They flopped come August, but June's success was sweet.

June was high season for PeeWee baseball. I biked to town for games, only to drop every ball hit to me and get picked off most times I managed to get on base.

Even though I never pitched, I was convinced that I would one day join Bert Blyleven in the Twins starting rotation. Back at the farm, I pitched against the door of the granary until it fell apart.

June was the time to relish newly-won summer freedoms, especially the freedom to sleep in until ten every day if you wanted, or to stay up late to listen to the Twins beat up on the Angels on the west coast.

Grown-up Junes seem less memorable than those of years ago. Yet, every now and then some sight, sound, or smell will bring me back to the timeless June days of childhood, and I wonder if they were really as dreamlike as I recall.

Saving Trees

Nothing punches me in the gut harder than when people tear down grand old trees without adequate reason. "Let's get rid of those old things," seems to be their motto, no matter how beautiful the old thing left them by the previous generations might be.

My love for old trees comes in part from a firsthand knowledge of how difficult it is to make them. Old trees are created by decades of time and good fortune. Most die or are killed before they reach maturity.

Nobody alive right now could plant an oak and reasonably hope to one day sit in its shade. An old oak, therefore, is priceless. You can't purchase one. You can't make one hurry up and grow. You can't move one in.

We are fortunate enough in this area to have beautiful old oak, as well as other trees which have somehow survived decades of wind, disease and human thoughtlessness. Are they not a gift which we should appreciate and preserve?

Okay, the old thing might be in the way for mowing. It might lean a little to the left. It might drop branches in a ninety-mile-per hour wind. It might even fall over in the next strong breeze, who knows. But to take out an old tree for those reasons is like shooting your dog because it might get a tick.

Yes, the pioneers had to clear the land to plant crops. You can't blame them for that. They had to live. But even though their rationale for cutting down trees is long gone, the clear-the-land impulse seems to live on.

Others can't seem to see beauty in a thing unless they've planned, planted and primped it by themselves. They destroy what is passed on to them in order to take full credit for what they put in its place.

Recently there has been a move to "redo" old cemeteries to make the stones straight. In many cases, old trees are taken down because they are causing a stone to rise, or because they obscure the writing on the stone.

At first glance, this may seem reasonable. At second glance, it is insane.

Who reads those stones, anyway? At most five people per year. How many passersby enjoy the big trees planted by the stones each year? Thousands.

Headstones are as dead as the people under them. Trees are alive. In many cases, they were planted by the people buried on the plot. What do you think the dead would rather have, a straight, clearly visible stone marker, or a grave shaded by an oak or an evergreen?

If a cemetery is to be more than just a storage space for dead bodies, trees are needed. Benign neglect often allows trees in cemeteries, especially the tall, narrow cedar, to develop into grand specimens. They are a living tribute to those six feet below, even if they block the writing on the stone.

Old trees in cemeteries and everywhere, like all old living things, deserve a measure of respect. They should never be destroyed without solemn deliberation.

Summer Storms

The summer storm season started with a bang last night. Much of our area awoke to over five inches in the rain gauge, water in the basement, branches down, big brown lakes in the fields.

As always, I left one window down on my pickup. The rain came sideways, so the whole cab is drenched. The windows will soon fog, and in two days the cab will smell musty.

This particular storm came from an odd direction. My house is used to strong northwest winds, but last night's wind came more from the east, and it pulled off some shingles. Apparently, every new wind direction exposes different weak spots.

The crowns of giant old cottonwood conceal an endless supply of dead limbs which shake loose during storms. The rotten big branches shatter on the lawn amidst the younger twigs. Oak are more stingy, seldom dropping branches larger than a golf club.

Despite the destruction caused by summer storms, many people just love them. Those who leave this area often mention summer storms as one of the things they miss.

Summer storms do put on a show. As the dark clouds gather, the gray billows swirl and boil in what weather people might call "tornadic activity." This is the stage in the storm where everybody gets up from the dinner table and runs to the top of the drive to get a better look.

With the first roar of the wind everybody scurries back

inside. The rain hits. A few hailstones bounce in the lawn. People fret about the garden, their car, the crops.

Next comes the lightning. If the storm hits in the middle of the night, it is fun to lie awake as the thunder cracks and rumbles overhead, from one horizon to the other. I used to count the seconds between the flash and the boom. Now I just try to guess which tree got hit.

Close lightning strikes terrified me as a child. Now, they amaze me with their raw power. Two summers ago, lightning hit a cottonwood next to my house and spread white wood splinters out 100 feet.

If the storm strikes in early evening and then passes over, the stage is set for a dramatic evening scene. As the sun lowers to the west, it casts an orange glow against the towering thunderhead to the east. The departing cloud silently flickers and flashes from the lightning within.

These enormous thunderheads, some of them which billow up to over 60,000 feet, are the closest approximation we get to mountains in this flat country. After driving in real mountains, I am thankful that we only have temporary ones which don't interfere with our straight roads.

Every so often you will see a rainbow. A rainbow's gaudy colors cause many people to run for their camera. Like most natural phenomena, however, a rainbow is probably best enjoyed without trying to capture it. Pictures are never as good as the real thing.

Nothing wrong with enjoying a storm, even one which does damage. There is nothing we can do to prevent storms from doing what they please, so we can just as well sit back and enjoy the show.

First Frost

We await the first frost. It might come at any time, and it might be both good and bad.

On one hand, an early frost kills off a good part of the garden and can damage some farm crops. On the other hand, an early frost kills off the mosquitoes and brings relief to those who suffer hay fever.

Let's hope humans never gain control over the weather. Can you imagine the fights if something as simple as the date of the first frost had to be determined by the legislature, or by the county commissioners?

The big money would push for a late frost. Cargill and ADM would lobby for late October to keep commodity prices low. Drug companies would want the hay fever season extended so they could sell more pills. Chemical companies would want to keep the mosquitoes buzzing as long as possible so they could sell more spray.

On the other side, the big gas companies would object to holding the frost off for too long. Prices might sink and jobs might be lost. Arctic Cat and Polaris would lobby hard for an early snow, as would the powerful ice-fisherman's lobby, formed to make sure the legislature keeps the ice on area lakes a foot thick five months per year.

Farmers would push for an early frost on everybody's corn but their own. Their demands would thus cancel each other out and be completely ignored, as usual.

Environmentalists would present the bizarre argument

that nature should be allowed to take its course. Such radical whiners would be told in no uncertain terms that this is 2001, please get your beads and smelly little hippie children out of our office or we're calling the cops.

To solve the frost date dilemma, lawyers from the early-frost companies would meet behind closed doors in a money-filled room with lawyers from the late-frost companies.

The compromise, pleasing to all parties with pull, would push the frost date quite late. Mosquitoes would require spray into late October. Bins would overflow with cheap corn. Allergy sufferers would pop pills right into flu season.

To make up for the revenues lost to early-frosters such as gas companies by the postponement of cold weather, the late frost, when it finally arrived, would immediately be followed by a good stiff blizzard and a month of forty below zero. Revenues would flow. Energy prices would soar.

The first frost agreement would disappear deep into the back pages of a popular tax rebate bill. The only debate would be: how much cash will it take to purchase the voters' silence on this issue and all others—three hundred dollars per person? A thousand?

No, let's be careful what we wish for. The ability to control the weather would just give humans more to fight over, more to decide in court, more decisions to be left in the hands of those with enough backing to twist things to their advantage.

Indian Summer

Since that October snowstorm, when it looked like we were condemned to an early winter, the northland has been graced by the rarest of weather boons, a true Indian summer.

The days are almost as short as they are going to get— yet, because the grass is still a rich green, it is almost bearable to have the sun set at five o'clock. When one can run around outside, one doesn't notice the short days.

A reprieve. A respite. A comeback. When the billows of white powder roared by the window three weeks ago, one would have thought autumn was over. But here we are, back in the fields, in our shirt sleeves with a second wind, milking a few more drops out of the season.

We know winter will come eventually. It always does. But there is something especially nostalgic and stirring about the unexpected good fortune of an Indian summer.

In my years watching baseball, nothing captured my imagination more than the old ballplayer, nearly retired, in the sunset of his career, who put it all together for one last burst of glory.

I remember when the great Tony Oliva, late in his career, with his knees reduced to jello, hit two home runs in one game. I was too young to remember Oliva in his glory days, but I could tell from the croak in broadcaster Herb Carneal's voice that night that seeing the decrepit Oliva hit two long ones brought back memories of something grand.

Baseball historians would point to creaky old Grover

Cleveland Alexander, long past his prime, soon to die a dissolute death, who, despite his questionable health and state of mind, stumbled to the mound in the ninth inning of the seventh game of the 1926 World Series to strike out the mighty Yankees and preserve a championship for the St. Louis Cardinals.

Ted Williams hit a home run in his last at bat. Babe Ruth hit three home runs in one of his last games. The mighty Nolan Ryan threw a no-hitter at age forty-six.

Winston Churchill was sixty-nine before he first became Prime Minister, the same age Ronald Reagan was when he was inaugurated President. Both had long before been written off as too old. Both were seen as dangerous. Reagan was viewed as an impulsive simpleton, and Churchill as a semi-crazy schemer. Both had suffered years of defeat.

But both Reagan and Churchill were underestimated and misunderstood by those who act intelligent for a living. Whatever one might think of their politics, the persistence and resilience of Churchill and Reagan, as well as their eventual triumph over their critics during the Indian summer of their lives, makes for a stirring story.

We know an Indian summer can't last. That is why it is so precious, and so appreciated. Winter will come, and soon. But the sight of a sunset over rich green grass in Minnesota in mid-November is as bittersweet and nostalgic to me as an unexpected cluster of home runs late in the season by an aging but beloved slugger.

Geese

There must be a major goose airport near my house. Dozens of cackling Canadians whoosh low overhead at all hours, sometimes in formation, sometimes in pairs, honking away with a noisy urgency which brings to mind a suburban mom on her cell phone in rush-hour traffic.

So human, the geese. Forming groups, holding meetings, chattering endlessly, following first this leader, then that, flying in enormous but apparently meaningless circles, only to land again where they last took off, in time for yet another meeting.

I don't know what they talk about at goose meetings. I don't speak Goosian, and interpreters are scarce. At first glance, it would seem that the availability of corn would be a likely topic, as would the decision over who will lead the V formation tomorrow.

Some of the geese are sure to be chomping at the bit to get up early and head north just after breakfast, while others just want to sleep in and hang out around here for a couple more days. There's a good cornfield here, and who knows what's up north? They say its nothing but canola once you cross the border.

But further contemplation leads me to think that the geese have developed extraordinarily effective coping mechanisms to deal with such conflicts within the flock.

For example, if the flock reaches an impasse on the should-we-stay-or-should-we-go issue, it seems that they simply split up. The up-and-comers up and go, and the dawdlers hang around and dawdle, with no apparent hard feelings between the two groups.

Such an elegant conflict resolution strategy separates

geese from humans, who would likely debate the issue for several hours only to table it until the next meeting, at which time nothing would have changed and everybody would just say the same thing over again, at which time the whole issue would be assigned to a task force, which would come up with the same recommendations as the last task force, which is that further study is needed in order to arrive at a workable consensus.

Geese, it turns out, have developed consensus-building strategies which put humans to shame.

For example, geese have largely solved the pressing issue of who leads the V by adopting a "rotational command" strategy. Finding two or four year terms impractical, geese instead change leaders several times per day, with each goose taking his or her turn leading the V as his or her energy permits.

Rotational command virtually eliminates the resentments and jealousies which inevitably arise against the lead goose when he or she is elected for a full four-year term. Such harping and infighting can seriously erode flock morale over the length of the term.

Under the rotational command system, each goose takes a turn at the top on a daily basis and sees firsthand that being lead goose is no picnic and that he or she probably wouldn't want the job full time even if it were offered. Honking in the ranks continues, but harping ceases.

Self-esteem problems disappear under rotational command, as each goose sees that he or she is a valued member of the flock and realizes anew each day his or her interdependence upon other flock members. Teamwork flourishes.

Motivational consultants are studying the goose leadership patterns for possible application in human situations. However, due in large part to ignorant human resistance to goose culture, such applications remain unlikely in the foreseeable future.

Humans apparently remain too addicted to treasurer's reports, new business, old business, elections of officers and four-year terms to adopt the effortless consensus-building strategies of the geese.

Fishing

Opening day of fishing season has come and gone. Whoopdeedo! Apparently opening day of fishing season is a big deal to some people. Men, women, old, young, rich, poor, sophisticated or crude, you never know who will be bit by the fishing bug.

The notion of sitting for hours on end in a boat waiting for a bite is just beyond me. And what is this "catch and release" deal? They reel in a big fish, weigh it, take a picture— only to throw the poor thing back in the lake? What's the point?

The first time I went fishing was in sixth grade. I caught six perch in the first hour, and my companions caught as many. But the rest of the day we just sat there. Not a nibble. I grew restless and bored.

As the sun sunk towards the horizon, I snuck over to the bridge and pulled up the stringer to have a look at the fish we had caught that morning. But the cable slipped through my fingers. The stringer with the fourteen fish slowly sank out of sight. My popularity rating with my fishing companions sank with it.

My next fishing experience came last winter. I decided I had to see what ice fishing was all about. There must be something magical about it, I thought, if thousands of allegedly sane people are willing to go to such lengths to stare down through a hole in the ice for hours.

So, I went out on the ice with an ice fisherman. The temperature was about zero. He had to carve out the hole again, and scoop out the ice chips and such. The scooping required that the door to the fish house be open. I stood there shivering and was no help whatsoever.

Finally we sat down to stare through the hole in the ice. The water looked like split pea soup. To provide a backdrop against which fish would be visible in the split pea soup, the fisherman peeled some potatoes and threw them to the bottom.

The main event was when a school of minnows darted through the soup, past the potatoes. Now it was split pea soup with raw potatoes and minnows, a dish which sounded even less appetizing than the green muck they served us in elementary school.

After the excitement of the passing of the minnows subsided, I got restless, just as I had in sixth grade. I had gained no greater understanding of the magic of fishing. I decided to leave before I did something stupid to antagonize my host. I had lasted one-half hour.

Although I will never be a fisherman, I do enjoy eating the fresh fish. The combination of a fish from Uncle Orville's hook with spices from Aunt Ede's kitchen is unbeatable. I enjoy fresh fish more than venison.

In fact, fishing generally strikes me as more dignified than deer hunting. Luring in a big dumb Northern to the dinner table seems less barbaric than blasting a fellow mammal into the freezer with a portable cannon.

In any event, my credentials as a Minnesotan are questionable. I was born here. I have lived here all of my life. But I don't hunt and fish. Do you suppose they will revoke my citizenship?

Deep Cold

Once a person's vehicle is warmed up, cold, clear weather isn't so bad. Below zero weather is preferable having it right around freezing when there's usually sleet, slush, ice and general misery. There is cleanliness and clarity to twenty below.

The scenery on the country highways is as crisp as the air. A trip in a warm vehicle at sunset on a bitterly cold, clear winter day is austerely scenic. The stark black outline of the leafless trees against the pastel shades of the winter sky provides a picture made to paint.

People change with the cold, too. The colder it gets, the more people sense that they are fighting a common foe. The kindness and camaraderie of a shared disaster kicks in, but without all the hassle of a flood, tornado or major blizzard.

The need to look nice goes out the window in below zero weather, at least for everyone but adolescents. Cap-frazzled hair is acceptable in all public spaces, including church. Boots so clunky that their wearer can barely drag them along become objects of envy.

Cold weather creates a different moral climate as well. For example, if somebody left their car running unlocked for a half-an-hour out at the lake in the summer time and it got stolen, most people would think that the victims were stupid enough to deserve it.

But at twenty below, parking lots outside of cafes, discount stores, grocery stores and churches in towns both big and small are filled with running cars, most of them probably unlocked. But you never hear of any running cars stolen in deep cold, at least not around here. That wouldn't be right!

In July, if a drunk person knocks at your door at three a.m. and walks in on his own claiming car trouble, you're liable to chase him off with a hunting rifle or maybe threaten to call the sheriff. When the same situation arises in below zero weather, the only proper thing to do is fix the poor sap some hot chocolate and visit with him until his buddies arrive to pick him up at sunrise.

Same holds true for motorists stranded on the roadside. I avoid them in the summer time. They'll survive. Somebody'll help them. They should have been better prepared anyway. But if it's ten below or colder, I don't think twice before helping.

Cold weather morality seeps into all areas of life up here, whether or not weather is an immediate factor.

As I clunked out of the cold into a hotel lobby in Fargo last weekend, I noticed a gathering at the front desk. An uptight-looking gentleman stood looking miffed as a cluster of three clerks huddled over some paperwork. Oh great, I thought, an argument over his bill.

The manager was called in. She pored over the bill as well. Things were serious. The bill was for several rooms, and looked to contain many, many phone calls. The manager furiously added it all up one more time.

"No," she finally said, "I am afraid that's the correct total."

"Okay," the man said, still skeptical. "It just doesn't seem like enough, and I wanted to make sure I wasn't shorting you."

"Nope," said the manager, "you're all taken care of."

"Okay, then," said the man.

Such an exchange could only happen in a very, very cold climate at a very, very cold time of year.

In the Name of Science

The shuttle accident brings to the forefront a class of people who don't get much attention until disaster strikes: scientists devoted enough to their work to risk their lives.

The shuttle crew knew the risks going up. The astronauts must have been aware that most commercial airliners have newer cockpit equipment than did the Columbia. They, more than anybody, knew that the margin of error when you hit the earth's atmosphere at sixteen times the speed of sound is miniscule. Yet, they went.

Are such space missions foolhardy? To many of us they would seem so, although a space mission is probably less foolish than Columbus's trip across the uncharted Atlantic in three tiny ships, or Lewis and Clark's plodding journey through thousands of miles of unknown terrain to the West Coast.

Explorers aren't normal people, whether they wrestle with the microscopic complexities of DNA or the endless mysteries of outer space. A curiosity few of us understand drives them, and drives them mercilessly.

Most fourth-graders are full of curiosity, but with few exceptions, their wide-eyed wonder at the world is boiled out of them by the time they reach their teen years. Maintain a passionate interest in science beyond your eighth grade project and you run the risk of hostility from peers and indifference from parents.

By adulthood, most human minds have frozen into place

on all levels. People do not wish to have their ignorant bliss interrupted by facts. New information, especially about some basic premise of our existence, becomes downright irritating to people just trying to pay the month's bills.

For example, nutrition and diet scientists are more unanimous than ever: to live longer and better, eat lots of fruit and veggies. Don't eat Twinkies. Eat whole foods. Eat lean meat. Cut out most sugar. The information is simple and it is easy to find. Yet more of us are fat, and fatter than ever before!

On a philosophical level, science has always been a threat to those with beliefs too brittle to embrace with equanimity and gratitude the wonders unveiled by scientific exploration and research. Their constricted view of the world might be a cause for pity if such folks weren't so nearly in the majority.

Poor church-going Charles Darwin! He bore no malice, yet thanks to the inordinate rage of those offended by his honest findings, Darwin has spent the century since his death wearing horns. Earlier on, the powers that be threw Galileo in the clink for having the gall to suggest that the earth went around the sun instead of the other way around.

The scientists aboard the shuttle mission were amongst a rare few whose passion for discovery survived both the teenage pressures of conformity and the adult temptations of lazy indifference. They broke through the innate human resistance to the unknown and the new, and accepted great personal danger to boot. They may well have been nerds, individualists, perhaps eccentrics, but they were at the forefront of our quest for knowledge.

We need more like them. We have been plopped into this magnificent, mysterious world. To not look around with awe, openness and unbridled curiosity at ourselves, at the universe, and at all living things is to die an early death of our own.

CHAPTER SEVEN

BACK HOME

Old Trucks

Temptation shows up when you least expect it. Last week, I was running errands in Fargo when I spotted a 1950 Dodge car in a furniture store parking lot, marked for sale, at a reasonable price.

It was perfect. The dark green original paint was tarnished with just the right amount of rust. From just outside the driver's side window, I could detect the delicious aroma of the musty seat cushions baking in the sun. The chrome-dome hub caps were unpolished but in good shape. The interior was unrestored, but intact.

My parents tell me that my love for the old rounded pickups and cars of the 1949-1955 era goes back to my toddler years. When I was two, my father pastored a church in Cavalier, ND. One of the parishioners, Ben Simon, kept one of those old, greenish pickups from the early 1950s on his farm.

Every time I saw Ben's old pickup, I would eagerly point and go gaga, or goo goo, or whatever vowel sound I was rehearsing that day. To this day, if I run into Ben, he gives me the report on his old pickup, which still runs. But it's not for sale. I've asked.

My favorite photo in my childhood album is of me as a third grader sitting on the bumper of a 1951 Ford truck that used to sit out near the woods on the farm. I loved that truck, even though it no longer ran, and the picture, taken on a golden fall afternoon, shows me as happy as I can ever imagine being.

When some of those old pickups were still on the road twenty years ago, a few people I ran into offered to sell me theirs for a couple of hundred bucks after they saw how much I wanted one. But that was when I was in college. Reality was harsh. Two hundred bucks could buy a semester's worth of textbooks. I decided to be prudent.

You know, I would never have missed those textbooks. I should have bought an old pickup instead. Now people realize their value, and the price has gone up.

So, when I saw this 1950 Dodge car in the parking lot of that furniture store, I was tempted to violate all of my tight-wad beliefs and practices and make an impulsive purchase of something I didn't need.

But practical thoughts intervened. I would probably have to haul the thing on a trailer. That would mean fixing the signal lights on the trailer and updating the tabs. Or, if the car was in running condition, I would have to get it collector plates. Hassle, hassle, hassle.

If the old car wasn't in running condition, I would have neither the desire nor the ability to fix the problem. When I stick my head under the hood of a vehicle, I am as lost as a Jersey cow in a library. No wrench adventures for me.

I wouldn't want to restore the car's body. It was already perfect–gently rusted, naturally aged. I would have no desire to drive the thing in parades, either. In fact, all I would want to do is park it out on the edge of my yard and let the cockleburs and quack grass grow up around it.

In that case, I thought, I can probably find an old pickup with a seized up engine in the woods somewhere around here for a lot less money. No use paying for a functioning vehicle when all I want is a lawn ornament.

So, I talked myself out of putting the 1950 Dodge car on my credit card. But if it's still sitting there in a couple of weeks, man, I don't know. It might be a good time for a mid-life crisis.

Cleaning the Garage

The obnoxiously early snowfall brought a rude halt to the fall work. I take the onset of winter personally, and as the snow piled up and drifted in, I stewed and paced inside.

To keep from falling into a bitter funk, I cleaned the garage, no easy task for a pack rat. Thank goodness for the woods. I dragged seven pickup loads of junk out back around the corner and dumped the stuff by the rock pile, just on the edge of the field.

Defunct computers. An ancient microwave, one of the originals. Printers. Furniture. Clothing. Magazines. Tons of tin cans filled with nails and screws of every size. Lamps. Old curtains and paint cans from the house's previous adminis-tration.

The grand finale, as the snow started to gather on the ground, was the disposal of a 1956 Allen church organ that I purchased in a weak moment, only to decide that it sounded too awful to keep in my house.

For the past five years, the monster has stared me in the face every time I opened the garage door, a daily reminder to think before writing big checks.

With great pleasure, I hooked a log chain through the hole for the volume pedal and around the base of the organ, put my pickup in four wheel drive, and slowly pulled out of the garage.

The organ stayed upright until it slid off the end of the slab, at which time it fell on its side with a huge bang, knocking the chain loose. I backed up, hooked it up tighter, and edged ahead.

The organ glided across the lawn, helped along by the slippery oak leaves, and left no marks on the grass. This was a real coup. It was going to be great to get rid of that thing. And without any help! I stepped on it as I approached the edge of the field.

As the organ followed the pickup off the lawn into the tilled soil, it rolled on its side. The keyboards dug a furrow into the ground. My pickup bore down. The instrument which had provided music for hundreds of weddings and church services became a one-bottom plow, with external speakers.

I unhooked the organ in a patch of cockleburs and triumphantly kicked it over on its back. Victory.

Then I got sad. I felt a little guilty, the same sort of guilt one gets when trading in a faithful car. So, just as I do when I trade vehicles, I paused for a moment of reflection, sort of to pay the instrument my last respects, before loading up the chains and heading back to the yard.

What a feeling! The garage sparkled. I swept away everything, even the cobwebs in between the studs, and surveyed my work with pride.

The garage didn't stay empty for long. The storm continued, so I decided to tackle the basement next. With the snow piling higher, the only place to put all of the junk from the basement was in the garage. Now the garage is full again, but with different junk.

In my book, that's progress.

New Cell Phone

Last fall for some reason I decided it was necessary for me to purchase a cell phone. After all, cell phones are so convenient–cheaper than a regular phone, especially with those 33,000 free weekend minutes per month–and you can call from anywhere!

Well, I never use the thing. It gathers dust in my glove compartment, just like the last cell phone I had, the one I turned over to the authorities after nearly killing myself and four people in an oncoming vehicle as I fumbled to dial while driving.

On this new cell phone, I place an average of one call per week. Not a one has been crucial. I have received perhaps ten phone calls in five months. None of them has changed my life. Not a one was even remotely important.

While in Arizona last winter, I took my new phone along on a hike to watch the sunset. Half-way up the trail, I pulled the phone out. The screen informed me that I had a new message. How exciting! It must be important, I thought. How lucky I am to have this cell phone.

But the trail was out of range. I was unable to retrieve the message.

So much for the hike. Forget the sunset. I knew I wouldn't enjoy myself knowing I had a new message waiting for me, so I ran back to my pickup and drove back into town.

Alas, I couldn't retrieve the message, even after I drove back within range of a signal. And more messages kept appearing! Three, five, now seven. Had somebody died? Did I win the lottery? Was the President in need of my counsel? I needed to know!

I called everybody I knew, trying to figure out who had been calling me. But nobody had called. Nobody had died. Nothing was wrong. And the President was surviving without my advice, as usual.

Turns out, I had the instructions wrong and was leaving a blank message to myself every time I checked for my messages. Sort of sad, going into a panic when you can't figure out how to listen to the blank messages you have left for yourself.

Note to the IRS: I deduct each month's cell phone cost. The cell phone is what keeps me in touch with my business. It is essential that I, the owner and grand poobah of a business, be in constant contact with my poor, helpless employees.

Reality: my poor helpless employees never call me. Not even to say hi. They didn't need me before the cell phone, why should they need me now? As a business expense, the phone has been a complete waste.

Cell phones are probably for very important people, or for people who need to look important. I am clearly not important enough to need one, and using the phone to look important only makes me look like a fool.

But please don't tell the IRS. I have to be able to deduct the remaining four years on this expensive contract.

Mosquitoes

The purpose of mosquitoes in summertime is to help us realize that there is something good about our long winters.

You forget about mosquitoes in January as you dream about working in the yard and raising a big garden next summer. Once they arrive, however, you suddenly remember why you never got around to those outdoor projects last year.

I am able to tolerate mosquitoes, as long as they stay out of the bedroom. But when I get awakened by an annoying buzz and a tickle on the temple at 4 a.m., it is time for battle.

Most northern bedrooms lack ornately patterned wallpaper. The reason for such bland decorating has nothing to do with taste. Northerners know that patterned wallpaper provides an ideal camouflage for mosquitoes. With white walls, the little buggers have nowhere to hide.

The problem with white walls comes after you kill the pest. If the kill happens after the mosquito has sucked of your blood, you now have a red splat on your white wall.

If you are real tired, it is tempting to go back to bed without cleaning off the spot. By morning, the mosquito's remains will have formed a permanent brownish stain that company will surely notice.

In that case, it is actually better to have patterned wallpaper, preferably something brown, so the corpse of the squished mosquito doesn't show and can just stick to the wall until you redo the bedroom. But you can't change wallpaper midstream, of course.

Not all mosquitoes are equally pesky. The big, slow, juicy ones with a low hum are an easy mark. If one lands on your face, you can usually get it with one gentle slap without breaking your nose, especially if it is weighed down by a large cargo of your blood.

The juicy ones smear on your face when slapped, but the smear usually disappears by morning, and the wet squish brings a satisfying sense of closure which makes it easy to get back to sleep.

Much worse are those nervous little mosquitoes which don't stay still long enough for your eyes to focus on them. You can't see them, but their high-pitched buzz reaches the ear from everywhere in the room. Sleep is impossible until they are killed, but killing them takes the sort of timing and accuracy only two cups of coffee can provide.

People who have lived here all their lives develop immunity to mosquito venom. The only bites which really bother them are those on the anklebone or the knuckles. But few people who still have their hearing are immune to the irritation of a mosquito buzzing around the bedroom.

Night-time mosquito-killing techniques vary. I try to let the thing land on my face and insert its stinger so it can't pull away so fast. Once the mosquito has dug in, bam, I hit my face so hard that it hurts. In most cases, I miss. Those little ones are quick.

At this point it is best just to turn on the light, find your glasses, get out of bed, and get the job done with a fly swatter. To locate the pest, however, your hearing must be perfect. Your reactions must be instant. And your walls must be white and empty of pictures.

When all else fails, and it often does, it is best to graciously admit defeat, leave the bedroom light on to keep the mosquito entertained, and spend the rest of the night on the couch.

Pancakes

Pancakes are my favorite food, although I don't believe in eating them after nine in the morning. They are a morning food. Ordering or making them at any other time of the day makes me feel as if I am still in pajamas.

However, it is perfectly proper to make up extra pancakes in the morning and eat them cold as a snack throughout the day. On the kitchen table in my grandparents house there usually sat a plate of cold cakes under a kettle cover. They didn't last long once I discovered them.

In New Zealand, you can purchase cold pancakes at most any bakery. They are rolled up with whipped sweet butter in the middle. I wish that idea would catch on here.

My cousin Lanette's Swedish pancakes are prize winners. She serves them with lingonberries. She lives in the Cities and has a large family, which causes two problems: for one, I don't get to eat her Swedish pancakes very often. For another: when I do, I have to share.

The worst pancake I ever ate was at the Bryant Lake Bowl in the Uptown neighborhood of Minneapolis. Their batter contained whole wheat flour, buckwheat flour, and several other virtuous but bad-tasting ingredients. The cake was awful. Nothing else on Bowl's menu is healthy, I don't know why they changed policy with their pancakes.

A couple of months ago I decided it was time for me to learn to make pancakes. I started with boxed mixes. They worked, but boxed mixes seemed like a cop-out, so I switched to making them from scratch.

My from-scratch pancakes were inconsistent and too bready. Plus, there were shiny black bugs in my bag of flour. So, I reverted to boxed mixes, and instead began to experiment with the type of liquid I added to the mix.

Buttermilk is best. In fact, I have come to believe that all cooking could benefit from a shot of buttermilk. A dash of buttermilk makes good pancakes, but it also makes killer mashed potatoes, scrumptious squash, tender chicken breasts, and tasty pork chops.

Back to cakes. Strawberry yogurt juice adds an irresistible fruity flavor. Soy milk makes smoother pancakes than cow milk. Adding a dash of oil or butter seems to make crispier cakes. Orange juice doesn't work at all.

Griddle temperature is vital. I turn the burner on three-and-a-half. That gets the right level of brown. Any hotter and you'll have a blue haze in your house until noon.

Making up the batter the night before is best, and it just gets better as the days go by. It is best to store the batter in the fridge or it can get crusty, especially if you run your furnace above sixty degrees.

I suppose this is ridiculous. I am passing myself off as some sort of pancake expert and I have been making them for all of two months. But in the interest of furthering pancake knowledge, I thought the least I could do was pass along the results of my research.

Poor Reception

The phone rings. You pick it up, but nobody's there. It rings again. You yell hello several times but nobody answers. It rings yet again a minute later, you pick it up, and all you hear is a bunch of static and snippets of a voice.

By now, you know. Somebody is calling from their cell phone while driving on some county highway where reception is spotty. The signal is strong enough to make your phone ring and force you up from the recliner, but not strong enough to allow conversation.

When this happens, I have learned the hard way that it is unwise to spit expletives into the receiver. The caller can sometimes hear you even if you can't hear them, and people tend to take rough language personally no matter how justified the outburst.

Now, I take my remote phone along to the recliner so I don't have to get up six times in three minutes to answer a call from somebody who isn't there, yet another example of technology causing a need for yet more technology to fight off the effects of the first technology.

When you finally do connect with a cell phone user, the reception can cut out without warning. This can cause grave misunderstandings.

I once took a call from a friend I hadn't heard from in a while. I apologized to him for not making it to his Superbowl party two months before. I was sure that he would understand, so I breezily said, hey, sorry about that, I was really tired and really busy, maybe next time.

A long, sullen silence. It was clear that he was deeply hurt, so I rushed to make amends. I said I felt bad for neglecting him, and suggested we get together soon, maybe for coffee tomorrow.

More silence. Wow, I thought, this situation is worse than I had suspected. It clearly required some full-scale groveling. So, I went on about how I had not been feeling particularly gregarious last winter and really hadn't been in touch with any of my friends, much less him, and that he shouldn't take it personally.

That did no good, which just made me mad. Good grief, I sputtered, if you're going to pout about it you can just forget it. I have no time for this passive-aggressive codependent behavior. Why can't you cut a guy some slack?

No response. So I went off about how I don't like football anyway and the thought of sitting on a couch for five hours watching all that overblown Superbowl hype gave me indigestion, which would only have been made worse by his wife's bad chili. I'd rather sit at home and floss my teeth.

About then I realized something was wrong. "Are you there?" I said. No answer.

Turns out, the phone had cut out sometime in the previous three minutes. I had just conducted a three minute argument with a dead phone, or so I hoped.

A few seconds after I hung up, the phone rang. It was the friend. He sounded calm. His cell phone lost its signal, he said, so he switched to the land line. He didn't bring up the Superbowl party, so I didn't either.

I didn't tell him that I had spent the past several minutes tearing him to shreds. The call passed without incident, although my blood pressure took a while to return to normal.

Thanskgiving Dinner

Sometimes just before Thanksgiving dinner somebody will suggest that everybody share one thing that they are thankful for. This suggestion usually arises after everybody has been seated, when the mashed potatoes, dressing, and gravy are already steaming on the table.

Everybody is starved. Further delay will just cause the corn to get cold and the gravy to develop a layer of scum. But nobody dares argue with the notion that a little suffering is necessary, probably to ease our guilt for eating such a sumptuous feast. We're commemorating the Puritans, after all!

The men look down at their laps, dreading their turn, hoping this is quick and easy and that nobody gives a sermon. The worst case scenario? Tears. Emotion. Drama. Please, let's just say the table grace and eat.

Little Jeremy announces that he is thankful that the Vikings won. Oh for cute! The humor breaks the tension, and brings much more laughter than such a remark would normally merit.

The tension resumes when Cousin Polly launches off on what she clearly intends to be a complete list of the good things in her life. There are only fourteen items. Sad for her, but fortunate for the rest of us.

The steam is by now barely visible over the mashed potatoes. The surface of the gravy has become dull and lardy. The lettuce is going limp.

Uncle Joe says he is thankful for his eight-point buck. That brings laughter, until it becomes obvious that he was completely serious, on the verge of tears. Somebody quickly says, "Well, that's nothing to sneeze at!" and Uncle Joe looks down at his lap.

Great Aunt Nora, over for the day from Sunny View, closes her eyes and announces, "I am just tankful for my helt." Her helt has been iffy for the past ten years, but this past summer was good, and everybody agrees that being helty is nothing to sneeze at, either.

Some smart aleck says he is thankful that we aren't having lutefisk, another says something about the roads being good, and another comments about the high hopes for this year's basketball team. Uncle Joe snitches a pickle, a clear indication that things are spinning out of control.

To restore order, Aunt Molly announces the table grace, which is sung in good harmony, and then the clinking of glasses and the clanging of dishes begin.

The mashed potatoes pour out steam again as soon as the outer crust is broken by the spoon. The gravy underneath the layer of lard is runny and warm. The corn is cold, but if you mix it with the potatoes as you are supposed to, it doesn't make a bit of difference.

After the first couple of bites, the trauma of the long wait fades. The food tastes so good and goes down so easy–it makes one feel truly tankful.

Christmas Goodies

So, the question becomes: what to do with all of the accumulated Christmas goodies that nobody wants to eat? What is it about Christmas that brings out the very worst in the world of sweets?

Candy canes. One per year is enough, but in December they appear by the dozen. For the forty-fourth year in a row, those squiggly rock candies worm their way into the bag of peanuts they hand you at Santa Day. People eat the peanuts, but the candy gathers at the bottom of the glass bowl with the peanut dust.

What is it with Christmas cookies? Why do they exist? Nothing beats a regular, generic chocolate chip cookie. Christmas would be fine with them alone. Yet, for some reason nobody can stick to plain old cookies in December.

In December, cookie makers bring out the food coloring for green and red frosting. Next come those little silver BB like things that pop out your fillings when you bite down on them. Red Hots. Colored sugar sprinkled on top. Layer upon layer of sugar of every form.

The worst cookies of them all are those rock-hard white things dipped in powdered sugar. While doing my research for this article, I finally discovered their name: Russian tea cakes. Or, if they are larger, Mexican wedding cakes. Who let that recipe across the border, anyway?

They should outlaw dipping things in almond bark. It has gotten way out of hand. Pretzels, potato chips, cheese curls–

what next, almond-bark dipped sardines?

Thrown on top of the homemade goodies are the store-bought, packaged Christmas candies. Chocolate-covered cherries are my least favorite. Has anybody ever finished an entire box of them? I doubt it. You squish the first one, red syrup drools out, and the whole box gets sticky. Pretty soon you just throw them away to save further trouble.

A few Christmas sweets could be good if we were allowed to enjoy them one at a time, apart from dozens of other kinds of sweets. For example, those peanut butter cookies dipped in sugar with a chocolate star pressed down in the middle are okay.

But you really have to dig to find the good stuff in those big boxes of Christmas goodies. And once one person discovers the little baggie which contains the good cookies, they're gone. If you don't move fast, you're stuck holding a baggie of Russian tea cakes.

They have recycle bins for everything else, why don't they put out some for Christmas goodies? They could let us think they will grind it all into bird food, or melt the stuff down to make next year's Christmas candy. In either case, recycle bins would take the edge off the guilt I feel for throwing away things which clearly were a lot of work to make.

Just listing all these gooey things makes me nauseated! And I haven't even mentioned fruitcakes, flatbread, rosettes, or krumkakke. I'll save them for next year. They'll be just as good then.

Christmas Letters

During the holidays, it is traditional to get in touch with old friends and otherwise lost relatives. But writing Christmas cards and letters usually means giving a report on one's life, a disconcerting prospect for those of us who have fallen a mile or so short of perfection.

Some leap to the task with glee, penning Christmas letters filled with dream vacations, high-achieving children, unbearably cute grandchildren, new additions, new cars, topped off by the inevitable little lecture on the True Meaning of Christmas.

The screed is photocopied, stuck with computer-generated labels, and mailed out like campaign literature, as if there is an upcoming referendum to determine Happy Family of the Year.

Such propaganda is understandable, I suppose. Nobody wants to hear the bad news, and wrapping one's life up into ten paragraphs of bliss with a big bow on top must be enormously satisfying to those who can pull it off.

But for most of us, the dishonesty required to pen such a letter, or the alternative unpleasantness of spilling the messy truth, makes writing a detailed Christmas report about as much fun as a colonoscopy on tax day.

Christmas is a time when people feel more pressure than usual to make their lives appear normal, sensible, happy, worthy of a Norman Rockwell painting. Never mind that the truth is always more complex and that such contrived happiness is usually skin deep.

Never mind, too, that the interesting people in the world

are generally those who couldn't put their lives into a Christmas letter if they tried, wouldn't if they could, and who really have no need to broadcast whatever happiness and normality they can muster.

Christmas can be an uneasy time for those who don't lead Christmas-letter perfect lives. It is a time when one is bombarded with expectations. Those who fail to fulfill those expectations are expected to explain.

You all getting together for the holidays? Maybe, if we feel like it. But not necessarily. We have no plans. Have you done your shopping yet? No, I don't Christmas shop until I feel like it and if I feel like it. You sent your cards yet? No, I think I'll send St. Patrick's Day cards instead.

Others once led letter-perfect lives, only to have reality get in the way. They could have written a shiny, happy Christmas letter, but instead they got divorced to save their sanity. They might have all gotten together, but Wilfred's drinking is out of hand again and it would just be a mess.

The perfect, happy Christmas gatherings often aren't all they are cracked up to be, either. Behind the pretty pictures lurk old resentments and rivalries, cutthroat competition between siblings, comparison of salaries.

The drive back to the suburbs is often a time to decompress, to say "Can you believe she said that?" or "Why does he have to control everything?" or "Aren't their kids obnoxious?" or "Could he be any more boring?"

Which is just to say that there are about a million ways to deal with the pressures of Christmas, ranging from trying to make everything look picture perfect to avoiding it altogether.

So, here's to a happy holiday to everyone, whether or not your life fits well into a Christmas letter. If it isn't always an easy time for you, you aren't alone. It can be a tough time for everybody, even those who take pains to make their lives look perfect.

Merry Christmas, and keep the faith.

Order Form

Copies still remain of Eric Bergeson's second book, *Still on the Farm*. To order either *Still on the Farm*, or additional copies of *Off the Farm*, please use the following form:

Name _____

Address _____

City _____

State _____ Zip Code _____

____Number of copies of *Off the Farm*
at $12.95 per copy
(shipping included)

____Number of copies of *Still on the Farm*
at $12.95 per copy
(shipping included)

Country Scribe Publishing
4177 County Highway 1
Fertile, MN 56540

Total for books $ _____

MN residents add
$.85 sales tax per book _____

Amount enclosed _____